Contents

Contents

Introduction

This book provides support and advice for all Foundation Stage practitioners – whether they work in settings in the private, voluntary and independent sectors or are in nursery or reception classes of primary schools. It will be of particular help to Foundation Stage managers and staff with management responsibility within any setting. It has been designed to offer a real 'value for money' programme of staff training covering a wide range of key elements for early years settings.

Accessible training

The training sessions outlined in this book can be easily organised within your setting without the need to find alternative venues. Each unit is practically based, with detailed guidance on how to lead staff through the training. No expensive specialist materials are required beyond those normally found in an early years setting. The activities focus closely on a setting's current work and planning. A high emphasis on the QCA publication, *Curriculum Guidance for the Foundation Stage* runs through the different strands of activities.

This book should enable all settings to build in a strong programme of staff development, which is an absolutely vital element for an effective and outward-looking team. It will help all Foundation Stage settings that are anxious to ensure that they provide up-to-date and relevant staff training, keep abreast of new ideas, offer different but successful approaches to teaching and learning, and address necessary new requirements.

Early years settings and Foundation Stage managers

Early years and Foundation Stage managers will want to be confident that their setting is both effective and efficient. They will be keen for parents to know that staff training is a regular feature of the setting's work. They will want parents to have faith that the staff who have charge of their children are well-qualified and professional in their outlook. This could be an important factor in parents' choice of a setting for their children.

Managers will also want to be sure that their setting meets all current regulations. They will want to take care to prepare staff for changes and new requirements, such as the introduction of the revised SEN *Code of Practice* and implications of the Foundation Stage Profile at the end of the Reception year, so that the setting ensures compliance. This requires a carefully planned programme of staff involvement and professional development. This book can, therefore, help to play a major part in supporting managers in these tasks.

Practitioners from all settings will want to have confidence that their provision and teaching is of a high standard and that they cover all the areas that are important for a quality early years experience for young children. They will want their managers and leaders to guide them through new procedures and to help them tackle new ideas. Practitioners will need a structured programme over time to be able to absorb new information, reflect on their own work and participate in developing new approaches within their setting. This book will provide a useful framework for managers and staff to address these issues over time.

OFSTED inspection links

Schools and settings who are liable for OFSTED inspections will want to demonstrate to inspectors that they have taken staff training issues seriously and that they have the evidence for a planned and delivered programme. This book can help managers and staff to prepare for their inspections in several ways. One complete chapter (Chapter 6 'Inspection issues' on page 79) is devoted to very specific staff preparation and training sessions for an expected inspection. In addition, all chapters are cross-referenced to OFSTED inspection issues. The training units offer a wide range of practical ideas for keeping evidence of important staff involvement (particularly reviews and evaluations of work and practice) that will be very valuable evidence for settings to present to inspectors. The evidence can be collected over time and many suggestions for how this can be easily organised are offered throughout the book.

Cost-effective training

Staff training can be an expensive business. To send staff out on courses during working sessions incurs cover costs or closure – which is particularly difficult for 'business' settings where income is affected. This is, of course, in addition to funding any fees required for the training itself. Although attending training courses outside of the immediate setting can be very useful and refreshing, closures and cover are not always popular with parents, and good-quality supply cover is often hard to secure. Therefore, it is often very useful and cost-effective to carry out staff training at the setting, during staff meetings and workshop times.

Below are some of the advantages of 'in-house' training offered in this book.

♦ Because of its nature, training can be tailored to the specific needs of staff or groups in the setting, for example, support staff or parent helpers.

♦ It can form a vital and manageable part of any setting's own self-review.

♦ It will help settings to work as a whole staff and enable them to adopt a uniform and consistent approach to new ways of working.

♦ It gives all staff a chance to participate, offer suggestions and share good practice.

♦ It provides staff with opportunities to relate training directly to the aims of the setting and the priorities for action, including OFSTED key issues for improvement.

♦ It acts as a catalyst for team building, with a chance for each member of staff to be valued.

♦ It helps staff to take responsibility for shaping the future of the setting – with real 'ownership' of agreed actions.

♦ It helps managers to keep an eye on quality control by ensuring that staff are aware of all policies and that they offer consistent, agreed practice whatever their roles within the setting.

Personalising the training

The activities within this book are designed to be flexible. They can be followed in self-contained sessions such as during after-hours staff meeting times. They could be linked together easily to make a longer 'Staff Training Day' programme. Settings can select the chapters – or specific activities – that best meet their circumstances, stage of development or concerns. The book can be dipped into to support a personal and specific need for training. Conversely, the book may be used as an entire course, planned over a long-term period and forming the spine of a setting's regular programme of in-service training. The choice will be down to each setting!

How to use this book

The training sessions are organised into eight chapters. Within each chapter there are six activities related to the overall theme. These have been chosen to cover a broad base of important and relevant areas for any setting to consider. The book contains photocopiable sheets for 40 of the 48 activities which will support staff tasks and make organisation easier. Many of them are designed to be used regularly after the training session as useful resources for your setting.

Each chapter's introduction will give you a clear idea of the scope of the activities and help you to decide if all, or only a few, are key areas for your own staff training. You may also find the 'Check-list' at the end of each chapter helpful in making a decision. In fact, these check-lists could be used as an interesting 'health check' activity in their own right! Look at the list of questions – that are related to the activities within the preceding chapter – and consider your setting's response. If you find that you are unsure, or give negative answers, go through the different activities and decide if a staff session on any of these would be helpful. These check-lists can also be used after you have completed the training programme to test out the increased level of staff knowledge and improved practice!

Organising the programme

The book aims to provide a flexible basis for staff training. You may dip into the sections which are particularly relevant to your needs at any given time.

Alternatively, you could choose to use it as a full staff development programme. This would provide a training schedule of approximately 18 months, covering one activity each week (and allowing for additional staff meetings to discuss internal arrangements), or the course could be spread over a longer period to take a more measured approach. However, as the chapters are free-standing, it would be sensible to decide the running order of how these will be followed in order to match your setting's priority needs.

Although the training sessions are designed for individual settings to use on their own, you may find it valuable to invite other settings to join with you from time to time to cover specific areas. This might also be a useful way of visiting different settings and finding out how others work, and the leaders could share the trainer's role together. This approach would be particularly suitable for all or part of a training day.

Many of the activities in this book are designed to take around one hour, to fit in with the length of time most schools and settings allocate for staff meetings and workshops. However, there are some variations, as some units are planned for only 45 minutes, and a few extend beyond the hour. A few of the units (where significantly more time is needed for staff to build on the initial training activities) require a further follow-up session. The recommended times are clearly indicated at the heading of each activity. There will inevitably be some minor differences in delivering the unit if your setting is very small – or conversely, where you have a large staff, when feedback times will obviously vary. You will need to consider this and make any small adjustments to your time-scales.

Staff involvement

Most of the activities have been deliberately planned to include all staff, to maximise staff awareness and involvement and, importantly, to help generate a consistent approach by all staff, irrespective of their roles. If you have part-time staff, you will need to consider when you organise your training – the units could be repeated if this is easier for you to organise. However, if you take this stance, be sure to feed the views and suggestions of each group back to the whole staff. An easier option might be to include all staff and put a range of activities together for a whole staff training day. For example, working through Chapter 6 'Inspection issues' on page 79 or Chapter 7 'Equal opportunities, Inclusion, Behaviour and Special educational needs' on page 92 would make a neat related package of activities.

For a few activities, the headings indicate the appropriateness of having managers, governor representatives, students and regular parent helpers present. When covering special educational needs, it is obviously essential to have the SENCO involved. However, settings can decide overall which personnel the training is most appropriate for.

All of the activities include a 'Further action' section with suggestions for how settings can follow up the training session, with practical strategies to reinforce staff development and benefit the quality of your general provision.

Chapter 1 Curriculum planning and delivery

This chapter focuses on training activities that will help your setting to review and strengthen the quality of its curriculum provision.
As a starting-point, the first activity in this chapter 'Auditing the Areas of Learning' on page 10 should help your setting to examine how well it covers the vital areas of early years learning. This will help you to ensure that you provide a broad, balanced and relevant curriculum for the young that children you cater for.

Introducing new ideas can sometimes be difficult and some staff can be resistant to change. 'Introducing new ideas successfully' on page 14 has been planned to help managers tackle this issue. The ideas present a 'safe' way to look at new ideas and channel staff reactions and energies positively!

Involving all staff
The importance of involving all staff as fully as possible in the planning, review and delivery of important curriculum aspects of your work is emphasised throughout the different units, especially in 'The planning cycle and systems' on page 12. It is also given prominence in 'Involving the team fully' on page 16 which is devoted specifically to encouraging whole staff involvement. All staff, whatever their role in your setting, have important contributions to make. They also need to be aware that their actions should reinforce your setting's overall development. It is important that your staff feel that they are a part of planning for future improvements and projects.

'Developing our provision for play' on page 18, particularly highlights the importance of play as being vital to young children's overall development. This activity is designed to help settings develop high-quality provision for play, linked closely to overall curriculum plans.

Building staff confidence
The activities in this chapter are aimed at building staff confidence through working together. Most tasks require whole-staff involvement in the review of current practice, as well as looking at ways to achieve agreed aims and outcomes.

The tasks in 'The planning cycle and systems' on page 12 and 'Planning for the future' on page 20 aim to enable all staff to contribute to an audit of your provision and to actively review the quality of your planning. Participation in the different activities in this chapter should help all staff to feel that they have a real role to play in the overall success of the setting.

Inspection requirements
The training sessions in this book have been planned to ensure that the Qualifications and Curriculum Authority's (QCA) current guidance for the Foundation Stage curriculum is repeatedly reinforced through a range of staff activities. Similarly, the training units are designed to meet the requirements of OFSTED inspections, both as a nursery school or class attached to a school, or as a private or independent setting receiving grant funding.

Auditing the Areas of Learning

Focus on the best ways to cover the six Areas of Learning within your setting

♟ Number of staff
All.

🕐 Timing
1 hour 30 minutes (can be split into two sessions).

What you need
A copy of the photocopiable sheet on page 121 for each member of staff (plus spare copies); six enlarged copies of the photocopiable sheet; yellow, blue and green pens; copies of current planning; copies of the *Curriculum Guidance for the Foundation Stage* (QCA) (available from QCA Publications, tel: 01787 884444).

Preparation
➤ Obtain several copies of the *Curriculum Guidance for the Foundation Stage*. Alternatively, photocopy the six Early Learning Goals and Stepping Stones grid sections from your own copy and highlight or mark the Stepping Stones in yellow, blue and green as illustrated in the actual document.
➤ Ensure that the staff bring their long- and medium-term planning notes to the session.

What you do
➤ Give an overall introduction explaining that the aim of the session(s) is to ensure that your setting's provision will cover all the necessary elements of the Foundation Stage, appropriate for the age range that you cater for.
➤ Spend approximately five minutes referring to the *Curriculum Guidance for the Foundation Stage*. Remind staff of the pattern of the six Areas of Learning and the general layout of the document. Explain that this does not prescribe an early years'

curriculum, but highlights the key elements that should be present in any setting's curriculum. Stress that your setting's curriculum needs to be personalised to meet the developmental needs and interests of your children, using your local environment, available resources and your community.
➤ Distribute copies of the six Early Learning Goals sections. Take five minutes to talk about these, emphasising that the Goals establish what most children are expected to reach by the end of the Foundation Stage – that is the end of their Reception year. Explain that by this time, some children will have exceeded the goals, whereas others – possibly the younger children in the year group – may still be working towards some, or all of them.
➤ Next, spend five minutes drawing attention to the Stepping Stones and the colour bands. Explain that, broadly, the yellow band is likely to be where most three-year-olds are operating; the blue band normally represents the developmental stage of learning for four-year-olds; and the green band will usually reflect the attainment of five-year-olds. The Early Learning Goals are the final Stepping Stone for the end of the Foundation Stage.
➤ Take a few minutes to talk about the range of ages in your setting and the appropriate range of Stepping Stones for your children. Highlight that the Stepping Stones are designed to give a useful ladder of progression from each stage to the

next – a way to build on previous learning. They should be used to ensure that your activities are planned to give the children opportunities to experience learning at the appropriate stage and age.

➤ Allocate the staff to work in six groups, one for each Area of Learning (depending on numbers present – in small settings you may have to cover only one or two Areas, and then repeat the task on other occasions until they are all covered). Allow 45 minutes for this task. Give each group member a copy of the photocopiable sheet. Ask the staff to work together and use their long- and medium-term planning for their allocated Area of Learning to complete the sheets. Each sheet should refer to just one Early Learning Goal. Have plenty of spare photocopiable sheets available, if needed.

➤ Explain to the staff that first they should fill in the appropriate coloured Stepping Stones for your setting's age groups (with the matching coloured pen). They should then identify and add your planned activities that show how the learning will take place. Remind them to look through all their planning, for example, many Physical development Stepping Stones can be supported through Creative development activities and vice versa!

➤ Display the enlarged photocopiable sheets around the room. Add an Area of Learning title to each sheet. Ask each group, as they discover any coverage gaps, to write in suggestions as to how your programme can be tweaked, adding the identified Stepping Stone and their proposed activities on to these charts in the appropriate colour.

➤ Bring the staff together and encourage each group to feed back

on their audit and, if necessary, their identification of any obvious gaps, with any suggestions for filling them.

➤ Make sure that all the gaps and activity suggestions are completed on the enlarged copies of the photocopiable sheet.

➤ At the end of the session, collect in all the photocopiable sheets and file them as useful evidence for inspectors of your curriculum coverage and analysis.

Further action

➤ Decide whether the long- and medium-term planning need any adjustment and, if so, carry this out. Circulate revised copies to staff.

➤ Discuss how these adjustments need to be taken into consideration for weekly/daily plans. It may be that you have identified minor gaps in coverage, or that there is insufficient emphasis or repetition of an area, such as when you have children joining at different times of the year. Your audit might, for example, reveal that the three-year-olds have only limited opportunities to 'tackle problems and enjoy self-chosen challenges' (Yellow Stepping Stone, Personal, social and emotional development). Your staff could now identify a focus in a play corner, offer more choices in tasks or set up specific activities or interventions that will lead to these intentions.

➤ Build in a staff review session the following term to discuss how any gaps have been successfully filled.

The planning cycle and systems

Invite staff to look at how to approach and improve your planning methods

🎔 Number of staff
All.

🕐 Timing
1 hour 15 minutes
(can be split into two
sessions).

What you need
A copy of the document
*Planning for Learning in the
Foundation Stage* (QCA)
(available from QCA
Publications, tel: 01787
884444); copies of your current
long-, medium- and short-term
planning, including daily plans;
flipchart; felt-tipped pens; large
ruler.

Preparation
➤ Read through the document *Planning for Learning in
the Foundation Stage* (QCA) and photocopy the different
examples of long-, short- and daily- planning models
(enough sets for groups of two or three staff). Clip these
together in sets, labelled 'A, B, C' and so on.
➤ Prepare a large sheet of paper, or flipchart, with the
following statements (drawn from the QCA publication on
pages 2 and 3):
1 '...a written plan is not an end in itself – it is the
planning process that is important.'
2 'A long-term plan is a way of ensuring that all six Areas
of Learning are given equal emphasis and that all aspects of
learning within the six Areas are covered regularly and
frequently. ...A long-term plan is usually designed with whole
groups of children in mind.'
3 'A short-term plan is based on the long term plan and
developed using ongoing observations and informal
assessment of the children. ...A short-term plan is usually
designed with individual or groups of children in mind.'
➤ Also add the following to your flip chart:
NB Most QCA examples also have additional detailed
daily/session or activity plans.

What you do
➤ Explain that the aim of the
session is to review current planning
and agree a standard approach
across your setting. The key test is
whether or not each person's
planning is clear enough to be
followed by someone who has to
step into their shoes.
➤ Refer to the *Planning for Learning
in the Foundation Stage* (QCA)
document and spend five minutes
going through the extracts that you
have written on the chart. After the
first point, ask 'Do we agree?' and
'What is the benefit of the planning
process?'. After the second and third
points, ask 'Does our planning match
these statements?'.
➤ Distribute the copies of the QCA
example material, one set at a time.
In small groups, ask the staff to study
each set, considering the long-term,
short-term and daily/activity plans
separately, and then with
'progression' in mind. Ask them to
discuss the usefulness of each layer
of planning and add their comments
to a large sheet of paper under the
headings 'Set A – long-term
planning'; 'Useful features'; 'Less
useful features'. Repeat for all the
sets. Allow approximately 20
minutes for this task.
➤ Come together for ten minutes
and ask each group to feed back. If
possible, decide which set and style
appeals most to the whole group.
➤ Now, work as a whole group for
approximately 20 minutes and
evaluate your own planning. Make a
note of any areas that need adjusting
or fine tuning.

➤ Remember **long-term planning** outlines WHAT IS TO BE COVERED AND WHEN

Check-list
♦ Does our long-term planning cover all the Areas of Learning?
♦ Does it take account of the children joining us at work?
♦ Does it link aspects of learning in an interesting way?
♦ Has it been personalised to show special events, visits and festivals?

➤ **Short-term planning** begins to outline HOW THE LEARNING WILL BE ORGANISED

Check-list
♦ Is it clearly based on the Stepping Stones?
♦ Does it show a range of adult-directed and child-initiated activities?
♦ Can we tell how the children will be organised? (For example, groups, specific individuals and different ages.)
♦ Are the roles of staff and helpers indicated?
♦ Can we see what specific resources/equipment for different activities are needed? (Such as, for sand play, water play, play areas outdoor play and so on.)

➤ Most of the QCA examples have **additional daily or activity plans**. Look at your own daily/ sesion plans. These should give the precise detail of the day's pattern of learning activities.

Check-list
♦ Is the pattern of the day clear?
♦ Do all the staff and helpers know what they are to do and when?
♦ Is support for targeted children shown?
♦ Are the learning objectives for different children clear?

♦ Are opportunities identified, and who will be responsible?
♦ Decide whether you need to develop your daily plans further and if so, note the areas for adjustment.

➤ Choose how to adapt your existing planning. If one of the models appeals to the group, draw a similar grid on a large sheet of paper and make any personal adaptations for your setting, Map next term's planning on to the new format. If you are happy with your original style, congratulate yourselves!

Further action
➤ If you want to introduce a new model for planning, this may require time to design. Select an introduction date for the new format at the beginning of the next cycle or term. Agree dates and arrangements for the changed format, including a series of staff sessions to convert the previous planning to the new style.
➤ Alternatively, draw up and circulate the agreed proforma to all staff. Share out the 'terms' on the old planning and ask specific staff to convert their allocated section to the new format, making any adjustments and inclusions as necessary. Circulate all the completed sections for the staff to consider and gather everyone together to make final adjustments. Together, check that all criteria are met (and that the process is 'user-friendly' for all future planning sessions) before the new style is introduced.

Introducing new ideas successfully

Encourage staff to find ways of presenting positive suggestions

✦ Number of staff
Four to 12.

⏱ Timing
Approximately 1 hour plus 30 minutes for follow-up meeting.

What you need
A copy of the photocopiable sheet on page 122 for each member of staff; enlarged copy of the photocopiable sheet; pens; black and red marker pens; large sheet of A1 paper.

Preparation
➤ Decide on a new idea or way of working that you would like to introduce. Try to arrange a visit to a setting that already uses a similar idea. Note all the main issues and benefits that you observe, or discuss them with the staff there. If this is not possible, think through your reasons for wanting to introduce a new idea. Read about the area and collect articles, quotes and so on to support your case. If the change is a national initiative or requirement, such as the revised *Code of Practice* for children with special educational needs or an urgent response to a health and safety issue, prepare brief notes on the issues and what has to be done.
➤ On the A1 sheet of paper, write the change or new idea that you want to introduce. Below, bullet point your reasons for why you feel that it is important.

What you do
➤ Refer to the A1 sheet of paper and spend approximately ten minutes explaining the new idea with expanded reasons as to why you think the change should be implemented, referring to any visits or research that you have made. Inform staff about any legal or national requirements that must be implemented. Despite any personal concerns, try to be positive – staff will be looking to you for leadership

and direction! Explain that you want to try the idea and need everyone's help to make it effective.
➤ Ask the staff to work in groups of about four. If your setting is small, pairs will work by doubling up the task, or work in threes and share the sections out. Give each member of staff a copy of the photocopiable sheet. Take a few minutes to talk through the sections and the roles of 'The Enthusiast', 'The Worrier', 'The Resource Manager' and 'The Organiser'. Discuss the different attitudes of each character and ask the staff only to think in this way for this task! Allocate the roles to the group members, being careful, wherever possible, not to give individuals roles that mirror their normal personality. The object is to make everyone think through issues in a fresh manner!
➤ Let everyone take a turn to lead discussions on their section and ask another member of the group to act as scribe and fill in the appropriate

box. For example, 'The Enthusiast' must only see positives and exciting possibilities, and lead the group to come up with only the advantages of the change. In contrast, 'The Worrier' should highlight all the negative elements to the group and let everyone discuss these – focusing on all the negatives and possible problems. The scribe should write these down as dictated.

➤ Similarly, 'The Resource Manager' needs to draw out discussions to decide all the current or new resources that will be needed to make the change work. This should include rough costings or whether needed resources could be made or borrowed, and if so, how this would be arranged. 'The Organiser' needs to bring out everyone's ideas for how organisational patterns of working or day-to-day arrangements must change. Where problems are unearthed, the group should try to offer workable solutions, or list areas that need further discussion and adaptation to make the new change work. Take approximately 30 minutes for this part of the activity.

➤ Bring the staff together for approximately 15 minutes to complete the enlarged copy of the photocopiable sheet. Encourage the staff to share ideas and discuss any issues. Write the agreed comments in each section in black pen.

➤ When all the sections have been completed, go back to the photocopiable sheet. Wherever there is a negative comment or problem, seek a positive way forward. For example, 'the parents will not like it' can be tackled with a decision on how to inform parents of all the positive benefits, and a plan to let them see it in action. Write the positive solutions in bright red pen!

Further action

➤ Write up the notes as a simple Action Plan (see the photocopiable sheet on page 125 as an example). Decide on a time-scale for the introduction of the idea and ensure that resources, organisation, staff deployment and responsibilities are clearly identified. Add a review date so that all the staff know that they will have a chance to evaluate the success of the change – or an opportunity to adapt things to make it work more effectively. Fill in as many sections of the Plan as you can and distribute these to all the staff asking them to check it and offer suggestions for improving the Plan or filling in the missing sections.

➤ Hold a follow-up meeting to go through the introduction programme and iron out any emerging snags. Decide on how, when, and by who, parents and other interested parties will be informed. Put the review date into the diary so that it is planned into your setting's schedule.

➤ This way of introducing new ideas can be used successfully for almost any intended change. It can be adapted by:
♦ Staff drawing cards for the different roles.
♦ Staff choosing their preferred role occasionally.
♦ Extending the roles to include 'The teacher's view'; 'The nursery nurse's view'; 'The rest of the school's view' and so on, as appropriate.

➤ You might find further reading useful – this can be found in *Six Thinking Hats* by Edward De Bono (Penguin ISBN 0-14-029666-2).

Involving the team fully

Bring your staff together to discover their star qualities!

☗ Number of staff
Four to 12.

⏱ Timing
Approximately 1 hour.

What you need
A copy of photocopiable page 123 for each member of staff; coloured pencils; pens; Post-it notes; flipchart.

Preparation
➤ Make a list of the most important priorities for your setting on the flipchart. These might be, for example, the key development points after an OFSTED inspection, or your own action plan. (See also 'Planning for the future' on page 20).

What you do
➤ Explain to the staff that the aim of the session is to develop ways of working that involve all team members and their unique contributions to the success of the setting.
➤ Give each member of staff a copy of the photocopiable sheet and inform them that this is their personal banner.
➤ Provide coloured pencils and pens. Ask everyone to write their name along the top edge of the banner.
➤ Highlight the small numbers in the four different sections of the banner. Invite the staff to draw pictures, signs or symbols in the different sections to represent the following:
♦ Segment 1: Something about yourself that very few people know.
♦ Segment 2: Something that you have done at work this term that you are really proud of.
♦ Segment 3: Something that you have done at home recently that you are really proud of.
♦ Segment 4: A personal motto or phrase that sums you up!
    Allow approximately ten minutes for this activity.
➤ When the banners have been completed, form small groups of two or three people and ask each person to hold up their banner. Suggest that the others in the group ask questions and try to guess what the signs, symbols and pictures show! Repeat until everyone has shared their banners. Spend approximately ten to 15 minutes on this, depending on the size of the groups.
➤ Now ask each group to nominate one volunteer to explain their banner to the whole group. Celebrate any unusual or previously unknown talents, skills and aspirations. (If the staff are shy, share your own banner first to get the ball rolling!) Take approximately ten minutes for this section.
➤ On the flipchart, make an anonymous list of all the interests, skills and so on that have emerged from the discussions and presentations. Ask group members to add any contributions that came from group presentations as well.
➤ Draw this activity to a close by focusing on the rich array of personal qualities, interests, skills and talents that team members have – and consider how this can enrich your team approach to all of your work. Collect in the banners and

display these in the staff room to remind the team of their uniqueness!
➤ Reveal the prepared list of your setting's priorities and spend approximately ten minutes going through these with the team. Highlight what has already been achieved and what is still to be worked through. Give prominent red ticks to all that has been successfully completed! Ask for any questions and clarify any concerns at this stage.
➤ Now concentrate on what still needs to be done. Ask the team to suggest any ways to help make progress, or new ideas and initiatives that could be considered that would help developments in the priority areas. For example, a priority might be to involve parents more in the work of your setting and, although some work might have already been done in this area, team members may have additional ideas to suggest.

Make a note of all the suggestions on the flipchart.
➤ For the remaining time, ask team members to think of a personal contribution that they could make towards each identified priority. Remind the group that they all have distinctive skills and interests that could be useful! Explain that ideas for contributions can range from making some themed dressing-up clothes or researching something on the Internet, to attending a specific course and sharing information with colleagues. Suggestions could also include undertaking to lead a working group on developing home-learning materials.
➤ Give out several Post-it notes to each group member and ask them to add their initials to each one. Ask them to fill in their ideas, sticking the labels to as many priorities or new suggestions as possible.

Further action
➤ Collect all the photocopiable sheets and collate the ideas, circulating these to all the staff. Reflect on the contributions, then have a personal discussion with each team member to discuss their ideas and how these could be developed.
➤ Support staff so that their personal contribution can be made. Try to find at least one idea that could be acted on. Perhaps pair like-minded staff together to share the work, or draw out small working groups.
➤ If a team member has only limited ideas, remind yourself of their interests and skills and partner them with someone else to give support. If someone has many ideas but these are fairly unworkable, retrieve the situation by finding at least one part of any idea that you can give them credit for and see if you can support their actions. Again, consider pairing or grouping with others to give recognition but practical help!
➤ Consider repeating the personal banner activity when new staff join your setting. You can also do this as an annually repeated activity, comparing the team's earlier banners and looking at how things have changed!

Developing our provision for play

Consider the importance of providing play activities for successful learning

⋇ Number of staff
Four to 16.

🕘 Timing
45 minutes.

What you need
A copy of the photocopiable sheet on page 124 for each member of staff; copies of enlarged photocopiable sheets; felt-tipped pens; small pieces of card; flipchart.

Preparation
➤ Go through staff planning and identify the different special play areas that are due to be set up, such as the garage, fire station, café, sand and water play and outdoor-play activities). If these are not clearly identified, select the main topics or themes that will be covered. Write each title and/or theme on separate small cards.
➤ Copy out the 'Children should experience' box (see right) on to the flipchart.

What you do
➤ Introduce the activity to the staff with a clear statement about the importance of play to children's development and that it is a major and natural vehicle for successful learning.
➤ Spend approximately five to ten minutes discussing the different types of play that the children should experience as part of good provision within your setting.
➤ Remind the group that because such a lot of staff effort goes into preparing good-quality play provision, the resulting level of learning should reflect this.
➤ Reveal the prepared chart and compare how many ideas matched, adding any additional ones that the group thought of!

Children should experience:
♦ explorative and representational play to help them make sense of their world
♦ play that will stimulate their imagination
♦ play that will let them try out different roles in various circumstances safely
♦ play that will encourage them to be creative and let them experiment with a variety of materials
♦ a good range of solitary, paired and group co-operative play activities
♦ activities that help them communicate ideas and feelings through play
♦ physical play that will be safely challenging and exciting
♦ opportunities through play to take risks, make mistakes and try to solve problems
♦ very active physical play and alternatively, opportunities for quiet and reflective play.
♦ Children need opportunities both to develop their own ideas without obvious adult intervention and also opportunities for adults to interact with them as they play!

➤ Give a copy of the photocopiable sheets to each member of staff and talking through the headings. Consider how one play activity can support learning in many areas.
➤ Now ask the staff to work in pairs or small groups. Show them the title cards and explain that you have drawn these from current planning. This exercise is designed to give opportunities to improve the impact of play activities.

➤ Let each pair select two title cards and then work together to complete a photocopiable sheet for each one. Allow 15 minutes for the task and then another ten minutes for groups to share their ideas with the whole group.

➤ For the remainder of the session, encourage the group to discuss and choose the most exciting ideas offered, contributing any further suggestions to improve the activity. Invite a scribe to write these down on an enlarged photocopiable sheet for everyone to see.

➤ As each photocopiable sheet is completed, invite volunteers to agree to make, collect together or arrange a working group, to produce any special resources that are required. Nominate one member of staff who will take overall responsibility for preparing any distinct play area space, such as setting up a corner for a hairdresser's salon or a travel agent's. This person will co-ordinate the use of the prepared resources and agree where the area will be positioned. Add their initials to the sheet. Ask others if they can help the lead staff by supplying any appropriate artefacts, such as rollers, hairdryers and travel brochures.

➤ By the end of the session, you should have some excellent detailed planning for each forthcoming play activity, and all the members of staff should have a clear idea of how they will each contribute to the children's learning!

Further action

➤ Add the final completed photocopiable sheets to your setting's planning documents. Let each staff member have a copy of the sheets, with their contributions clearly identified. Keep the list of all the agreed play activities, with approximate dates of implementation, and lead staff identified, and display this in the staffroom to help staff keep an eye on time-scales.

➤ Collect suitable storage receptacles for the resources that will be produced. Large, labelled boxes are useful, as well as large drawstring bags made from fabric remnants, and both are easy to store. Put a laminated or plastic-covered copy of the appropriate planning sheet into each play resource pack for future reference. Let the staff begin to prepare agreed resources to extend the children's learning. Where possible, involve parents and helpers in collecting and collating resources, and also ask the local community to help.

➤ After each planned play activity has taken place, ask the staff member who took the lead on its preparation to conduct discussions with colleagues on how effective it was in extending learning. Encourage them to make a note of any adjustments that need to be made in the future, such as additional resources, space, types of planned interventions and extra support or challenges that could be built in to benefit younger or older children.

Check-list

♦ Did the activity stimulate the areas of learning we hoped for?

♦ Were the resources appropriate?

♦ What other resources would be useful?

♦ Was the activity stimulating and exciting enough?

♦ How did younger/older children respond to the activity?

♦ What adaptations are needed to ensure that all groups of children can participate fully?

♦ Which types of adult interaction/intervention were most successful?

Planning for the future

Focus on the most practical ways to structure your future plans

Number of staff
All.

Timing
Two 1-hour sessions.

What you need

Pens; green, yellow and red Post-it notes (traffic-light colours!) or coloured paper and Blu-Tack; three sheets of white A1 card; felt-tipped pens; a copy of photocopiable sheet on page 125 for each person;

Preparation

➤ Draw coloured edges around the sheets of A1 card – one green, one yellow and one red. Title the green card: 'Go! What we do well'; the yellow card: 'Get ready! What we are working on now' and the red card: 'Stop! What we need to improve'. Have OFSTED reports, monitoring reviews or previous action plans available for reference.

What you do

Session 1

➤ Explain that you are going to do a 'traffic-light' activity to involve all the staff in deciding what needs to be planned for future development.
➤ Give out the coloured 'traffic light' sheets of paper or Post-it notes and invite the staff to work in groups of three or four. Ask them to think about all areas of your provision and, if necessary, refer to the reports and previous Action Plans to jog their memories. Let them take ten minutes to talk about this, then write on the green 'Go!' sheet, everything that they can think of that is going well in your setting. Remind them that this can be to do with the curriculum, work with parents, relationships, special needs, the community, teamwork and so on – anything that they are pleased with in any aspect of their work.
➤ Repeat the task using the yellow 'Get ready!' sheet to list everything that you are currently working on to improve learning, standards and provision. Again, think widely and include things such as 'improving the garden area', 'developing newsletters' or 'seeking funding'.
➤ Repeat again with the red 'Stop!' sheet, discussing every area of provision that the members think needs to be improved. For example, 'A lack of gross motor physical activities in inclement weather.' Include all comments on the list. If the staff can think of suggestions to make this happen, add these, too. For example, 'The entrance is too congested – move the storage units to the parents' room'.
➤ Place the large cards around the room and ask the staff to fasten their traffic-light sheets to the matching one.
➤ Take approximately 15 minutes to hold up each card in turn and read out the group's contributions. Discuss these and ask for agreement on the green and yellow cards, ticking each one, as appropriate. For any differences of opinion, ask the staff for their reasons and let the group make a decision to keep the sheet there or remove it. For the red card, ask the group to give each suggestion a number from one to ten, with one being the most urgent and important area.
➤ Rearrange the red sheets in order of importance and go through them

again, discussing and writing on the sheet when it should be done, for example, 'Immediately' or 'For the next parents' meeting' and so on.

➤ For any remaining time, return to the yellow sheets and mark with a star, any current developments that continue to need attention. For example, you may have introduced a new system of home visits recently, but this needs to be continued to see if it has made a positive difference.

Check-list

♦ Have we included all the issues from our OFSTED inspection?
♦ Have we given these top priority for attention so that they have been tackled ready for the next inspection?
♦ Have we got too many priorities?
♦ In our setting, with our staff numbers, can we realistically achieve these priorities?
♦ Select only the most important and make sure that it is a manageable number!

Session 2

➤ Come together and quickly remind the group of the red and yellow priority order lists.
➤ Give a photocopiable sheet to each person and spend approximately five minutes talking through the headings, ensuring that everyone is clear about what needs to be included.
➤ Ask the staff to work in groups of three or four and share out no more than the top eight red sheets among them. Explain that they will have 30 minutes for this activity. Ask each group to write one 'red' task that needs to be done in the appropriate column. Let them discuss ideas of how the task might be achieved and decide which ideas would be most

useful, adding these to the correct column. Encourage members of staff to complete as many other columns as possible, leaving blank any they are unsure of.
➤ Start a new sheet for each 'red' task and repeat the activity.
➤ Take approximately 20 minutes for each group, in turn, to present their ideas to the rest of the staff. Encourage questions and further suggestions to complete the columns and use emerging ideas to fill in as much of the sheets as possible.
➤ In any remaining time, tackle the 'yellow' tasks in the same way as the 'red' tasks.

Further action

➤ Collate the individual sheets and distribute them to all members of staff. Have a further session completing the time-scales and personnel who will lead and support the various activities.
➤ It will be helpful if you have pencilled in some preliminary suggestions for this. Look very carefully to make sure that you are not trying to do too many things at the same time. Space out the workload over a year or eighteen months. Seek volunteers to lead – or oversee – each action, and identify support from other staff, yourself, or external sources, such as teacher mentors or trainers.

A check-list for your setting concerning the issues raised in **Chapter 1** Curriculum planning and delivery

➤ Are all the staff familiar with the *Curriculum Guidance for the Foundation Stage* (QCA)?

➤ Do we use this frequently for reference and ideas to check that we cover all the Areas of Learning?

➤ Do we use the Stepping Stones to ensure that we match work to developmental stages for the age groups that we teach?

➤ Have we reviewed our programme to ensure that we cover all required elements of Personal, social and emotional development?, Communication, language and literacy?, Mathematical development?, Knowledge and understanding of the world?, Physical development?, Creative development?.

➤ Have we identified what we do well and where we need to improve coverage?

➤ Does our planning give frequent opportunities to cover all the Areas of Learning?

➤ Does our long-term planning link areas in an interesting way that is personalised to our setting?

➤ Does our short-term planning show how learning will be organised?

➤ Do we plan to meet the needs of children of different ages, full and part-timers and those joining our setting at different times of the year?

➤ In reception classes, does our summer term planning ensure that the literacy and numeracy sessions are gradually and fully introduced?

➤ Do all the staff plan in the same way and how are support staff involved in the process?

➤ How do support staff and helpers know what is expected of them?

➤ How do we introduce new ideas? What examples of adopting new ideas do we have?

➤ Do staff react positively to new ideas or do we need to work at this aspect?

➤ How are new members of staff brought into the team and valued?

➤ How do we involve them fully in our setting's overall aims and development?

➤ How do we keep our team involvement fresh and enthusiastic?

➤ Do we ensure that play is given sufficient focus in our provision?

➤ Have we developed a range of imaginative play activities with clear learning objectives?

➤ How do we ensure that all the staff and helpers know how to extend learning through our play activities?

➤ Have we reviewed our play resources, and do we have plans to make or obtain new ones?

➤ Is everyone involved in reviewing our setting's provision?

➤ How do we ensure that all the staff have a clear picture of our setting's aims and what we need to do to achieve them?

➤ Do we talk about our overall aims and vision enough with the staff and helpers?

➤ How do we help all the staff to share the same vision for our setting?

➤ Do we have written plans with actions, time-scales and involved personnel clearly identified?

➤ Do we find time to review how these plans are working and make any adjustments?

Chapter 2 Observation and assessment

This chapter shows how staff in early years settings can develop their observation and assessment skills.

Observation and assessment are vital tools in identifying children's stages of development and determining starting-points for their continued learning. Staff also need to be able to check children's progress carefully and accurately so that they can plan specific tasks that will consolidate or extend children's learning.

Establishing systems

Settings need to develop simple and manageable assessment and recording systems that enable a range of staff, and parents, to contribute effectively to the assessment process. 'Manageable systems' on page 24 is concerned with helping settings to establish their own assessment systems, using a range of practical suggestions.

Planning and record-keeping

'Observation techniques' on page 26 deals with the importance of developing very precise observation techniques, so that the assessment of children's responses to different situations and learning is planned into a setting's programme. The need to use assessment information to plan further tasks to enable individuals and groups to build on previous learning is also stressed.

'Staff involvement' on page 28 is designed to help all staff focus on the different roles that they may have in contributing to the assessment process. Due emphasis is given to the clear identification of intended learning for groups and specific individuals. This unit would also be useful for regular parent helpers and students.

'Recording initial profiling' on page 30 is concerned with supporting schools and settings in establishing their initial records and profiles on individual children, and building on their current practice. Schools are encouraged to involve their overall assessment co-ordinators and Foundation Stage managers in the training because there are particular implications for them in introducing the revised arrangements and timing of the Foundation Stage Profile requirements.

Involving parents

The vital importance of parents being partners in the assessment process is reinforced in 'Sharing with parents' on page 32. The role of parents is highly emphasised in the QCA guidance materials and is duly examined in OFSTED inspections. Parents are the first educators of their children, and developing a productive relationship is essential. In this training unit, staff are given opportunities to rehearse potentially sensitive parental discussions and to refine their communication skills in a safe situation.

Finally, on page 34, all the issues in using assessment information to promote learning are brought together. In very practical tasks, staff can share real assessment observations and consider a range of ways that the learning for specific children can be developed further.

Manageable systems

Consider how to review and improve your assessment systems

꩜ Number of staff
Two to all.

🕐 Timing
Approximately 1 hour.

What you need
All your current assessment records and materials; large space to set them out for easy viewing; *Curriculum Guidance for the Foundation Stage* (QCA) (available from QCA Publications, tel: 01787 884444); flipchart; felt-tipped pens.

Preparation
➤ Photocopy page 24 of the *Curriculum Guidance for the Foundation Stage* (QCA) with the explanatory boxes, beginning, 'Skilful and well-planned observations of children' for each person.
➤ Copy the following extract from page 16 of the same publication on to the flipchart:
Principles for early years education
Practitioners must be able to observe and respond appropriately to children.
This principle requires practitioners to observe children and respond appropriately to help them make progress. This is demonstrated when practitioners:
♦ make systematic observations and assessments of each child's achievements, interests and learning styles
♦ use these observations and assessments to identify learning priorities and plan relevant and motivating learning experiences for each child
♦ match their observations to the expectations of the Early Learning Goals.

What you do
➤ Explain to the staff that the aim of the session is to review and, if appropriate, improve your assessment systems. Spend approximately ten minutes going through the 'Principles' chart, explaining its source document.

Ensure that all the staff are clear about the importance of assessment in young children's learning.
➤ Discuss the three main points and ask the staff to share real examples of how this happens currently in your setting.
➤ Now distribute the photocopies of page 24 of the *Curriculum Guidance for the Foundation Stage* (QCA) to the staff. Spend approximately 15 minutes reading through the sheet together. Read each statement and then its accompanying 'example box'. As before, ask the staff to give examples of how this is currently undertaken.
➤ On a chart, make a note of 'What we do well' and 'Areas that need development'. For example, 'Home visits and pre-entry visits give us good information from parents' and 'Difficulties in recording what we have assessed in general activity times'.
➤ Now ask the staff to spread out your own assessment records and systems. Working in pairs, ask them to go through it together, checking that it matches the general principles above, and making a note of any strengths and weaknesses they perceive. Take 15 minutes for this task, with a further five minutes reporting back to the whole group. Add their findings to the chart.
➤ For the remaining time of the session, concentrate on the 'Areas for development' list. Invite the staff to suggest ways that these areas could be tackled – or ways that further research into solving any problems could be followed up, such

as visits to other settings, contact with a teacher-mentor, further reading and so on.

➤ Work your way through the practical ideas check-list below for any ideas that might help!

Check-list

♦ Have a ring-binder for each child to include all records and assessments from home and school, plus dated examples of work.

♦ Include all home information, for example, contacts, family members, health issues, the child's special interests and so on.

♦ Provide special file sections for each of the Areas of Learning. Add a list of the Early Learning Goals and Stepping Stones, highlighting the most appropriate.

♦ Invest in a camera for your setting – digital if possible – and display each child's photograph prominently on the cover of the ring-binder.

♦ Take photographs frequently of individuals and groups working on different activities to add to the files. Add photographs or reduced-size photocopies of work, contributions to displays, construction and role-play work.

♦ Regularly share the file with the child and his or her parents to talk about what the child has achieved and what he or she is learning to do better. Display the files in an attractive and accessible manner, but stress the personal and private nature of them.

♦ Encourage parents to contribute information about their children frequently.

♦ Plan plenty of opportunities when the children can independently select work for their own files. Ensure that the children are always with you for parents' meetings.

♦ Give each member of staff a roll of adhesive labels and suggest that they wear them about their person at all times! This will enable them to jot down any significant observations, date them and then stick them straight on to the appropriate file pages. This will prove to be a great time saver and all the staff can contribute!

♦ Have a rolling programme of target children, for example, two or three each session. Note where the children are likely to be working and ask all the staff to make a note of any significant observations.

♦ Pass all the notes to the child's teacher or group leader at the end of the session. Have brief discussions with the staff on any relevant matters.

Further action

➤ Arrange any follow-up visits or contacts, or seek out examples of assessment organisation ideas. Set a date for a further staff meeting to share ideas, to finalise your own system and to decide an appropriate introduction date.

➤ Using a diary, plot out the key dates for implementation of your ideas, such as new approaches to home visits and parental meetings in order to share information, or designing new, parent- and child-friendly information sheets or colour-coded file sections.

➤ Obtain the necessary files, resources and storage arrangements and organise the required administration. Ensure that you communicate to parents and carers how your system will work and what their role and access to it will be. Discuss with the staff any potentially sensitive issues such as split families, difficult health issues and so on. Talk about how these will be handled consistently.

➤ Ensure that all the staff understand the new system and then run it for an agreed time, perhaps two terms. Review its success and make further improvements.

Observation techniques

Focus on ways to share best practice and develop observation techniques

👥 Number of staff
All who will be involved in observation.

🕐 Timing
45 minutes.

What you need
A copy of the photocopiable sheet on page 126 for each member of staff; enlarged copy of the photocopiable sheet (as large as possible!); the next day's planning; pens; flipchart; felt-tipped pens.

Preparation
➤ Prepare a large chart with the following questions in one colour ink:
♦ Who was observed?
♦ Which activity was observed ?
♦ Was it planned or incidental?
♦ What was observed?
♦ Which Areas of Learning were involved?
♦ What learning took place?
♦ Were adults involved?
♦ Which other children were involved?
Add in another bright colour:
♦ What can we learn from this observation about the child's developmental stage?
♦ How do we use this information to help the child's learning?
♦ What should we plan next?
➤ Then fasten a sheet of paper over the last three questions so that they are hidden from view.

What you do
➤ Explain that the aim of the session is to share best practice and to focus on developing rigorous observation techniques to improve learning.
➤ Ask the staff to work in pairs. Let them spend ten minutes in pairs, with each partner taking turns to share two different activities that

they have observed in the previous week, and how different children reacted to these tasks.
➤ Ask the staff to identify the Areas of Learning that were covered, reminding them that activities often support more than one Area, for example, emergent writing that takes place during role-play supports Physical development as well as Communication, language and literacy! Use the 'Check-list' on page 27 to guide discussions.
➤ Produce your prepared question chart. Now take approximately ten to 15 minutes (depending on staff numbers) for the pairs to feed back to the whole group one of the observations that they discussed, responding to the uncovered questions.
➤ Reveal the covered questions on the chart. Explain to the staff that an important part of observation is noting what stage each child is at with his or her development. The staff need to carefully focus on what the child can do, what they say, how they interact with others and how they react in different, particularly unfamiliar, circumstances. To really discover what a child knows and understands, it might be necessary to engage in the activity with the child and ask, 'Why?' and 'What if...?' questions to support their observations.
➤ Stress to the staff that equally important to making the assessment through observation, is deciding what the next steps need to be for the child and how they will plan to meet these needs. This is applicable

to the most advanced children, those making steady progress or those whose progress is limited. It is also appropriate for those who have identified special needs.

➤ Revisit the examples that the pairs offered, but now ask all the staff to suggest activities and approaches that will enable the targeted child to make progress. For example, if a boy who was observed modelling with play dough appeared to find difficulty using small tools, how could he be helped to improve this skill? What activities and support might he be directed to in future? What choices might he be given? Take approximately 15 minutes for this activity.

➤ Give each member of statff a copy of the photocopiable sheet. For the remainder of the session, ask them to work in their pairs and look at the next day's planning. Let each person decide on one activity that they will observe closely and, if appropriate, name up to two children that they will focus on. Ask the staff to complete their photocopiable sheets in readiness for the observation.

Check-list

♦ Where was the observer positioned?

♦ How many children could be successfully observed simultaneously?

♦ Were the children aware of the adult's presence? If so, did this affect the observation in any way?

♦ Was the observation made through adult intervention? If so, how did the observer react in order to gain useful assessment information?

♦ What would you do differently next time to improve the quality of observation?

Further action

➤ Make copies of the photocopiable sheet for all staff. If possible, laminate these for permanent reference and inclusion in any planning files. If appropriate, reduce the copies to handy A5 size. Laminated copies could be repeatedly used by observers (including parents and helpers if the sheet has been prepared in advance) if an appropriate water based felt-tipped pen or china-craft pencil is used.

➤ Arrange to carry out 'Using assessment for learning' on page 34. Establish a regular programme of assessment by encouraging the staff to carry out one detailed observation each week on a rolling programme of children. Use the photocopiable sheets and ask staff to include them in their planning files – this is good evidence for OFSTED inspectors to show how assessment informs planning. Where the children have been observed and particular activities planned to help them make further progress, repeat observations could focus on how well learning has been extended.

➤ Put copies of the photocopiable sheets in the children's files to show assessment and progress. Share these with parents, who can also add their own observations based on information from the home or after they have carried out agreed supporting activities themselves. For example, by letting the child help to lay the table, practising pencil skills or encouraging them to play co-operatively with others.

Staff involvement

Help your staff to understand their roles in assessing children's learning

✿✿ Number of staff

All staff – regular parent helpers and students could also be invited if they contribute to the setting's normal supervision and support in the assessment process.

🕐 Timing

1 ½ hours – can be split into two sessions.

What you need

A copy of the photocopiable sheet on page 127 for each person; pens; A3 cards; next week's planning; flipchart; felt-tipped pens.

Preparation

➤ Invite the staff to bring their next week's planning with them. Prepare the following headings on the flipchart:
Activity
Group or individual (add name)
What we want the children to learn
Individual special needs support required
Key vocabulary
Key questions to ask

What you do

➤ Explain that the aim of this session is to clarify the roles of all the staff in observation and assessment, and to reinforce that all adults have key roles to play in children's learning.
➤ Take ten minutes to remind everyone that observation and assessment is a complex area in an early years setting where so many different activities are going on –

often simultaneously! To obtain an overall picture of each child requires focused observation under different circumstances. Talk about the different types of activities and staff roles during sessions. Ask each member of staff to share with the others a key role that they played (either planned or by accident) in helping the children to learn during the previous week. Ask them to explay what they did and say what the outcome was.
➤ Lead discussions for approximately another ten minutes by asking what the complementary roles of staff should be in assessment. In what ways, if any, should the roles of support staff be different from teaching staff? What part should visiting staff, students, helpers, parents and other agencies play in assessment? Make a note on the flipchart of any issues raised.
➤ Return to the issues raised and spend another ten minutes or so considering any concerns or negative comments. Ask the group how they could resolve these and turn them into positives. For example, someone may be concerned about issues of confidentiality. You may suggest that this could be resolved by passing all the information through a named member of staff and by your setting sharing a very explicit policy or code of conduct with all concerned. Make a note of any emerging points for action or further consideration.
➤ Give out copies of the photocopiable sheets and ask the staff to work in small groups, of say two or three, ensuring that there is a

mix of different types of staff in each cluster. If possible, also mix the groups so that staff can have the opportunity to work with colleagues who they do not usually work closely with. Give each group 15 minutes to complete the 'jigsaw' and comments.

➤ Take approximately ten minutes for each group to feed back their ideas to everyone. If necessary, make a note of any issues that require further thought at another time.

➤ Stress to the staff that the key to teaching or supporting groups or individual children is knowing exactly what knowledge, skills and understanding you are trying to extend. This could be new learning, such as sharing a book to discover how badgers live, or consolidation and reinforcement (letter formation practice games). Highlight that to assess progress precisely, the staff need to know what the intended learning – or learning objective(s) – of any activity are. This might include distinct vocabulary, using particular equipment or making choices confidently. If these aspects are clearly identified and shared with different members of staff being responsible for a group or activity, then they should be able to make useful assessments to feed into the overall picture.

➤ For the remaining time, give out the A3 cards and ask the staff to work in their normal planning groups. (If this is not possible, let them work in small groups.) Show them your prepared 'activity card' layout. Ask them to look at their forthcoming planning and choose an activity that each member of the group will be responsible for during the next week. For each one, ask them to discuss and complete the card together and keep it neat ready to use alongside the chosen activity.

Further action

➤ Use the activity cards as planned and ask the staff who supervised the activity to consider how well the children in the group learned what was planned for them.

➤ On the back of the card, ask them to make any assessment comments or any further work that needs to be done to extend learning. For example, 'AJ quickly learned the vocabulary and used it to talk about his model' or 'LPS lacked confidence on big apparatus and needs more opportunities to develop this'.

➤ Raise the results at the next planning session and see if these children can have access to activities that will give them more challenge or support. Also pass the completed cards to the responsible staff for inclusion in the children's files.

➤ Prepare similar activity cards for the following week's schedule and extend this to include cards for parents, helpers and other visitors to use at your setting, as appropriate. Arrange to be available to briefly discuss the parents thoughts with them and collect the cards before they leave.

Recording initial profiling

Concentrate on the main issues of Foundation Stage profiling

❀❀❀ Number of staff

All with responsibility for recording progress.
In school settings –
Assessment
Co-ordinators and
Foundation Stage
Managers.

◷ Timing

Approximately 1 hour
15 minutes (depending
on your setting).

What you need

Two copies of the photocopiable sheet on page 128 for each member of staff; two more photocopiable sheets enlarged to maximum size; pens; current recording documentation; good-sized space to display documentation for easy viewing; current guidance on the Foundation Stage Profile (available from QCA Publications, tel: 01787 884444); arrangements; flipchart; felt-tipped pens.

Preparation

➤ If you are in a school setting, you will need to prepare two flipchart sheets. For the first sheet, write a title: *Foundation Stage Profiles*. Then rule four columns on the flipchart with the headings:
Requirements
When?
Who?
Issues for organisation
➤ For all settings title a chart: Initial Assessments. Then rule four columns with the headings:
Implications
When?
Who?
Issues for organisation

What you do

➤ Spend five minutes reminding the group about the Foundation Stage Profile, that takes place towards the end of the Reception year. Discuss how this will affect your setting.

➤ If you are a school setting and will be involved in the arrangements, take another 20 minutes to share the current guidance for the profiling and work across the flipchart headings, making a note of key areas for attention. Particularly highlight the dates when this assessment needs to be undertaken. Consider carefully how the assessments need to be carried out, which staff will need to cover them and what affect this will have on your programme and classroom arrangements. Let Foundation Stage Managers and Assessment Co-ordinators take concerns and organisational implications to the school Senior Management Team for resolution of any issues that affect the whole school.

➤ For all settings, take a few minutes to explain that it is vital for all practitioners to know each child's 'educational starting-point' as they enter any setting, in order that they can be guided towards activities that will build on their experience and developmental stage.

➤ Give each member of staff two copies of the photocopiable sheets. Talk through the headings together. Then name a very recent admission to your setting, preferably a girl. Invite the staff to fill in all the 'balloons' on the first sheet, writing comments about the child's stage of development when they started at your setting, based on their own observations. Ask them also to complete the sections 'Other useful information'. Allow about five minutes for this task. Then distribute the second sheet and give the name of a very different child, preferably a boy. Allow the staff five minutes to repeat the exercise.

➤ Now spend approximately 15 minutes to let the staff feed back their comments for each child, in turn to the rest of the group. Encourage questions and discussion, then write down the agreed views on the enlarged copies of the photocopiable sheet.

Checklist

Stress:

♦ the need for good observation skills and clear evidence in the six Areas of Learning;

♦ where you should seek further useful evidence (parents and carers, other agencies, previous settings and so on);

♦ how many sources of evidence give a more complete picture;

♦ how many people can feed into the assessment process and how this needs co-ordinating;

♦ confidentiality and sensitive issues.

➤ For the remainder of the time, ask the staff to work in pairs or small groups to look at your current initial assessment. Talk about how the information is gathered and identify what works well and where the system could be improved.

➤ Discuss together how the initial information is shared with all the staff, how it is accessed for planning purposes and how it is used to check the progress the children make as they move through the setting.

➤ Talk about how this information is shared with parents and carers and other agencies such as social services or special needs support services.

➤ Make a note of any areas that need further attention to be dealt with at another session.

Further action

➤ Review your entry profile information sheets and make the design attractive and user-friendly for parents. Many settings use a set of sheets, designed with a special unique character to make these appealing and less formal (for example, 'St Mary's Mouse'!). Ask the staff for ideas and, if possible, encourage a volunteer to create some lively illustrations to include on your sheets!

➤ Arrange to visit other settings and ask for examples of how they organise initial profiling. Ask your teacher-mentor for suggestions of where to contact co-operative settings or to give you examples of other ways of obtaining and collating this information.

➤ Consider consulting parents on the ways that you involve them in gathering initial information about the children. Ask them about the ease of completing any pre-entry information sheets, about your systems for involving them in discussions, including home visits and/or setting meetings, before their children enter your setting. Also seek their views about arrangements for sharing information together as their children progress through your setting.

➤ Consider setting up a small consultative group of parents and staff members to discuss pertinent issues. This might include sending home simple questionnaires (that the group might be involved with designing) to seek wider views.

➤ Hold further training sessions for the staff following the first three activities in this chapter to develop assessment skills and procedures further.

Sharing with parents

Develop the communication skills of those staff who work with parents

👪 Number of staff
All staff who work with parents.

⏱ Timing
Approximately 1 hour.

What you need
A copy of the photocopiable sheet on page 129 for each member of staff; pens; A6-sized cards (one for each person); flipchart; felt-tipped pens.

Preparation
➤ Write all or some of the following scenarios on to separate A6-sized cards.

1 Anxious young mother, first child about to enter early years education – very unsure and nervous.

2 Very harassed mother, several younger siblings, keen just to get the eldest off her hands for some of the day.

3 Over-protective mum, not looking forward to parting with her daughter but thinks it is the correct thing to do.

4 Single dad has a child-minder to look after his child while he is at work, finding it all a bit confusing.

5 Well-experienced mum, all her children have come to your setting and her youngest is now due to start.

6 Parent, fairly new to Great Britain and with limited English, accompanied by a relative, unfamiliar with early years settings, but wanting to place her son.

7 Working mum has taken time off work, with a very boisterous child who she feels 'is very bright and needs lots of stimulating activities'!

8 Carer, fostering a newly placed only child, is keen to let her experience a good early years setting, particularly learning to play with other children.

➤ If you have specific examples pertinent to your setting, write these on the appropriate number of cards. For example, if you serve a particular minority ethnic area, have a high proportion of children in care, have parents who work or children with special needs, reflect these in your scenarios.

➤ Head the flipchart: *Sharing with parents* and add two columns below titled *Dos* and *Don'ts*.

What you do
➤ Explain that this session is aimed at enabling all staff who gather information and share discussions with parents to develop their communication skills.

➤ Spend five minutes reminding staff of your setting's arrangements for meeting parents before their children enter your provision. Discuss the sort of information you want to collect at these meetings and how you currently go about it.

➤ Distribute the photocopiable sheets and spend approximately five minutes talking through the headings of the information that you want to collect from parents of new entrants, as well as the information that you want to give to them.

➤ Next, invite the staff to work in groups of three, if possible. Give each participant a card and ask the staff to read, but not to share, their scenario at this stage.

➤ Encourage the staff to think in role and spend approximately five minutes writing three questions or concerns that they think their character would want to raise at an initial meeting with setting staff.

➤ Ask the groups of three to take turns to play the role of the parent, the interviewer (completing the photocopiable sheet) and the observer. If you have to work in pairs because of staff numbers, role-play the parent and interviewer.

➤ Spend approximately five minutes on each interview plus five minutes feedback time with the observer making comments on how they felt it went. Encourage the staff to reflect upon how they think it felt for the parent and also from the practitioner's point of view. Use the check-list below to help focus the discussions.

➤ Repeat the activity to enable all the staff to play all three different roles.

➤ Bring all the staff together again and spend approximately 15 minutes on this last activity. Encourage the staff to feed back the key points for making the parental contact and interviewing productive.

➤ Then invite everyone to suggest ideas and complete the flipchart of 'Sharing with parents – Dos and Don'ts'.

Check-list

◆ How did the interviewer make the 'parent' feel comfortable at the beginning?

◆ Was there good eye-contact from the interviewer?

◆ Was the tone friendly but professional?

◆ How did the interviewer try to help the 'parent' feel at ease when being questioned about their child?

◆ How were any tensions dealt with?

◆ Was the interviewer's communication clear and helpful?

◆ What did the body language indicate?

◆ Did the interviewer read the signs and adapt their approach appropriately?

◆ Did the parent have time to raise concerns and ask questions?

◆ How did the interviewer deal with these?

◆ Did the interviewer gather the information they needed?

◆ How was the interview concluded?

◆ How did each party feel about the interview?

Further action

➤ Type up the flipchart and circulate it to all the staff as a reminder for any future interviews.

➤ Repeat the activity using the same parent cards, but this time give out a further set of cards that raise a difficult or sensitive issue after the child has been attending your setting for a short time. For example, a child's disruptive behaviour; difficulties with requested access – or frequent unannounced visits to the setting by an estranged partner; some observed physical or learning problem and so on. Discuss what your setting's procedures should be in these circumstances and who should be informed early on about any concerns.

Using assessment for learning

Focus on using assessment information to promote children's learning

♟ Number of staff
All.

⏱ Timing
45 minutes.

What you need
A copy of the photocopiable sheet 'Using assessment information to promote learning' on page 130 for each person; pens; next week's planning; flipchart; questions from 'Observation techniques' on page 26; felt-tipped pens.

Preparation
➤ Carry out the training activity 'Observation techniques' on page 26 of this chapter.
➤ Prime two or three more confident staff to be prepared to share the results of their planned observations and ask all the staff to bring their completed photocopiable sheets to this session.

What you do
➤ Take approximately five minutes to explain that this is a follow-up session on honing observation skills and how to use this information to inform the next stage of planning. Remind the staff of the work that they did together on observation techniques and of the task to follow-up that session with planned observations of different children.
➤ Draw everyone's attention to the chart of questions (see 'Preparation' on page 26) and refresh your staffs' memories by reading these through. Stress that you are sharing experiences openly and honestly and that a team approach will help everyone to build on best practice or tackle problems together!

➤ Allow approximately ten minutes for the two or three primed volunteers to share the results of the observations that they made after that session. Encourage other staff to ask questions about the process and invite someone to make a note on the flipchart of any emerging techniques that worked well, or issues for further consideration.
➤ Spend another 15 to 20 minutes (depending on the number of staff involved) encouraging the rest of the staff to take turns to feed back from their photocopiable observation sheets, answering the questions on the chart as they do so. Let them suggest how they planned, or intend to plan, further activities, or how they will organise groups to extend their target children's learning. Encourage the staff to indicate if they are unsure of what the best next steps might be, or, if they are in a support role, to ask the person responsible for planning for their considered ideas.
➤ Even where the planned follow-up learning strategies have been good ideas, encourage all the staff to make alternative suggestions of suitable follow-up activities, or how specific teacher-direction and interaction may help. Stress that there are many equally effective activities that enable the children to consolidate or extend their learning. Aim to have as many examples as possible in order to generate a 'tool bag' of different ideas and tasks.
➤ Encourage ideas that the parents could be involved in at home that would also support learning well.

➤ Ask the reporting staff to identify any problems that they encountered as they undertook the observations, and ask everyone to suggest solutions.

➤ Now distribute the new photocopiable sheet on page 130 and read through the 'planning wall' headings together.

➤ For the remaining time, ask the staff to work together in pairs or small groups. Ask them to each nominate a child and the area that he or she needs extra help with.

➤ Then, consulting the next week's planning, let the staff help each other by suggesting ways that the planned activities could be used or adapted to meet the learning needs of each named child.

➤ Invite the staff to complete their own copy of the photocopiable sheet, leaving the 'Outcome' stone empty.

➤ Reassemble as a whole staff and let one or two volunteers feed back their intended actions.

Check-list

◆ What do I want the children to learn or improve?

◆ How will this activity give them opportunities to extend learning?

◆ Is the task focused enough?

◆ How will I direct the child to the task?

◆ Can I put an element of choice into the activity and still promote the same learning?

◆ Will the child work as an individual or with others? If so, will the child be part of a group of children all of whom are around the same developmental stage?

◆ If adults are to be involved, what should their role be?

◆ Are there any key questions that they should ask?

◆ Is there any key vocabulary that

they should use to help the children understand or learn new terms?

◆ Are any specific resources required?

◆ What will I observe if the learning has taken place or improved?

Further action

➤ Ask the staff to organise the activity that they have chosen and try to observe their target child. If support staff are to be involved, ascertain how they will focus on the intended learning and how they will feed back to the teacher or responsible staff member.

➤ After the activity has taken place, complete the 'Outcome?' stone. If improved learning has been evident, congratulate yourselves! If more attention needs to be paid to consolidating learning, or the activity did not appear to be as successful as you had hoped, remember that young children do not always learn at the same rate and that progress can reach a plateau at times.

➤ Leave a little time and involve the child in another activity that will give him or her another chance to make progress.

➤ Put the completed sheets in each child's personal file as an assessment record that can be shared with parents and carers in due course.

➤ Repeat the activity, using the 'planning wall' sheets, from time to time to check on children's progress. This can be especially useful to keep a record of your setting's actions to help children with special needs and as an assessment over time of their development – or otherwise.

A check-list for your setting concerning the issues raised in **Chapter 2** Observation and assessment

➤ Are all the staff familiar with the *Curriculum Guidance for the Foundation Stage* (QCA) requirements for effective assessment and planning for children's learning?

➤ Do we use a simple, manageable and effective assessment and recording system?

➤ Can we improve it without making it too unwieldy?

➤ How can all our staff contribute to assessment effectively?

➤ How do we ensure that all the children are regularly assessed and their progress is recorded?

➤ Have all the staff been trained in observation techniques and does everyone carry it out consistently?

➤ Are we gathering a bank of 'activity cards' for the different tasks that we provide that help the staff to identify and assess key learning aspects?

➤ Do we have individual files for the children?

➤ Does our initial assessment profile show the educational starting-point for the children?

➤ How is this information gathered and who contributes to the profile?

➤ Is it attractive and user-friendly for staff and parents, including photos and other devices such as our setting's character mascot or logo?

➤ Does it include, where appropriate, information from other agencies?

➤ How do we share it with parents and include their own comments and observations?

➤ Do we share it with the children and include any of their comments?

➤ How have we adopted the new Foundation Stage Profile requirements and how does this feed into our overall school Assessment Policy? (School settings.)

➤ How do we use the information from other settings as the children transfer to our school? What liaison do we have with 'feeder' settings? Have we sent them a copy of our initial assessment profile and discussed this with them? (School settings.)

➤ How do we involve parents fully in the assessment process?

➤ What is our programme for parental consultations and is it extensive enough?

➤ Which staff (key staff, teacher only, named contacts, all) liaise with parents and how are parents' comments formally recorded during their children's time at the setting?

➤ How do we encourage parents to help their children learn at home, and how do we use any resulting information sensitively?

➤ Have we developed appropriate activities for parents to use at home? How might we extend these and link them with individual children's needs?

➤ Do we regularly target children for observation on a rolling programme?

➤ How do we share all the emerging information, successes and concerns with all the staff?

➤ Does our assessment lead to planned adjusted activities that meet the needs of children of different ages and abilities?

➤ How clear is the information we send to the providers of the next stage of our children's education?

Staff-training activities   *early years* **training & management**

Chapter 3 Maximising resources and the environment

This chapter will help you to look at your setting's general resources with fresh eyes, enabling you to recognise the potential of what you already have within and around your accommodation and in the wider environment.

The activities in this chapter should help you to identify areas for development and will also provide suggestions for planning to improve resources and general provision. This might mean budgeting where necessary, or considering possible use of the immediate locality to support young children's learning in an exciting and imaginative manner.

Checking resources

The first activity on page 38 engages the staff in a practical audit of what is immediately available to the children. It involves checking your current resources and sorting out those that can be usefully renovated and those that need to be updated or removed. It provides a good opportunity for staff to work together to streamline materials – a real chance to 'cut the clutter'!

The vital importance of learning through quality play activities is the focus of the activity on page 40. This session puts aside time for all the staff to consider together how a range of fresh and engaging play activities can be developed simply from the areas that you plan to teach. The sharing aspects of this activity make this unit a good, ongoing, team-building activity as well as improving the range of stimulating play materials!

Extending learning

In the activity on page 42, the staff are helped to understand the difference between directed and independent work. It looks at creating an appropriate balance between staff-directed activities and those that the children initiate themselves, as well as providing suggestions for extending learning through skilled adult intervention. 'Displays with impact' on page 44 concentrates on ensuring that staff time and energies spent on creating displays are rewarded with the maximum learning for the children. The emphasis is on developing your intended displays to meet this aim.

Outdoor play

The quality of outdoor play has been identified by OFSTED inspections as a common area of weakness. 'Outdoor learning' on page 46 enables the staff to consider how outdoor play opportunities can be creatively extended for your setting. Although it looks at developing physical skills, it also highlights the chance to extend the children's learning through all six Areas of Learning in the Foundation Stage curriculum.

Finally, the activity on page 48 focuses on staff working together to develop productive use of the locality, particularly in extending learning through Knowledge and understanding of the world. It gives valuable time to review possible extensions to your programme and can go on to involve the staff in taking a lead in exploring new developments.

Auditing your resources

Concentrate on reviewing your resources and learning environment

👥 Number of staff
All.

🕐 Timing
Approximately 1 hour 30 minutes (or two sessions of 45 minutes).

What you need
A copy of photocopiable sheet on page 131 for each pair of staff; pens; Post-it notes or similar; flipchart; felt-tipped pens; nine sheets of A1 paper; large bin; large box or container; sticky labels.

Preparation
➤ Title each sheet of paper to match the headings on the photocopiable sheet. Copy out the check-list of questions on page 39 on to the flipchart.
➤ If some resources are not readily accessible to the staff, arrange them where they can be seen and examined, for example, around the setting's tables.
➤ Label the bin 'Out' and the box 'Repair or renovate'.

What you do
➤ Explain that the aim of this session is to review the learning environment and resources provided by your setting, and to pin-point how these could be developed further.
➤ Make a strong statement that ensures the staff understand that every part of your provision (including external areas, waiting zones and cloakrooms, all work and 'home' areas, all displays and wall spaces, toilets, outdoor-play areas and so on) help to shape a child's experience and learning. Spend ten minutes identifying 'What is *our* learning environment?' and considering all the aspects of your setting.
➤ Now invite the staff to move to the entrance of your setting and wait together as if they were visiting for the first time. Divide the staff into pairs and ask them to walk around the premises together. Encourage them to stop repeatedly, and crouch to get a child's eye view of their surroundings.
➤ Ask the staff to make a note of any inviting areas that promote an eagerness to learn, and conversely, areas that require some attention to maximise positive impact. Take approximately 20 minutes for this.
➤ Come together for 15 minutes and ask the whole group to feed back their findings on the current quality of your learning environment.
➤ On the flipchart, make a note of any areas that require improvement. Decide how these improvements can be made and who will lead developments and when. If a larger project is required, such as some alteration to layouts or minor building work, make a note that this will need to be explored further for future planned improvement and try to ascertain a date for further exploration, feasibility and costing.

If you are splitting the session in two stop here, otherwise continue.
➤ Ask the staff to work in pairs, preferably with a colleague that they do not always work with. Give each pair a copy of the photocopiable sheets and spend approximately ten minutes reading through the headings and discussing ways in which resources affect a high-quality learning environment. Read through the check-list of questions below to promote discussion.

Check-list

♦ Do we have enough resources available to meet the needs of the children (consider their ages and stages of development) in our setting?

♦ Do we have resources to promote learning in all areas of the Foundation Stage curriculum, including Stepping Stones?

♦ What resources support indoor activities well?

♦ How good are our role-play resources (artefacts and dressing-up clothes)? Are they exciting and imaginative? Is there sufficient variety?

♦ How good are our outdoor-play resources? Are they challenging and engaging? Is there enough variety? Are there any shortages? What is needed?

♦ Are resources in good condition? What needs repair? What needs replacement?

➤ Show the staff the labelled bin and the box. As they undertake their survey, ask them to bring any broken, dirty, damaged, 'tired' and/or unsuitable resources back and put them in the appropriate container. If they are in doubt, let them place the resources in front of the containers and ask the group to decide.

➤ Display the large titled sheets prominently around the room. For approximately 20 minutes, divide the staff so that they visit at least two of the areas identified. Ask them to complete the appropriate boxes. When they have done this, ask them to copy their 'Needs and improvements' on to a Post-it note, and then stick it on to the corresponding sheet. In this way you should collect very useful ideas for replacement or development in every area of your provision.

➤ Finally, come back together as a group and review the audit that you have just undertaken. Invite the staff to decide on any queried resource disposal, then be ruthless and throw the poor-quality items away!

Further action

➤ Use the staff 'Post-it notes' of required improvements and resources to draw up a needs list. Go through this list and identify all those resources that you must purchase when funds allow, or that could be made or improvised. For example, dressing-up clothes could be made by some volunteer parents, and cheap charity-shop clothes could be adapted for use. Ask parents to donate toys, jigsaws and games that their children have outgrown or items such as gardening materials.

➤ Could large equipment be shared with another setting and used by rotation? For example, telephone boxes, shop fronts or construction apparatus could be easily shared with another setting if you adapt your planning. You would only have to store it for part of the year and items would always emerge fresh and exciting for your children!

Extending learning through play

Focus on extending children's learning through quality play ideas

⚏ Number of staff
All.

◷ Timing
Approximately 1 hour, with a follow-up session of 1 hour.

What you need
A copy of the photocopiable sheet on page 132 for each member of staff; red and blue pens; planning for future work; empty storage boxes; sticky labels; sheets of A4 card; flipchart; felt-tipped pens.

Preparation
➤ On one sheet of paper on the flipchart, draw a plan of your setting, indicating areas designated for different play activities, such as home play, role-play, sand play, water play, outdoor play, construction and so on, matching a specific period of your planning.
➤ On another sheet of paper, write out the two aims of the session:
1 'To give everyone a chance to reflect on the importance of play in the children's development'
2 'To plan the most imaginative and exciting forms of play that will stimulate the children's learning'.

What you do
➤ Refer to the aims on the flipchart, spending a few minutes reading through them.
➤ Make a strong statement about the need to maximise the potential of planned play activities to keep them fresh, exciting and attractive to the children. Stress the need to consider each play activity and reflect on how learning could be extended through providing different resources or a sharper focus.
➤ Show your setting's plan and talk the staff through the different

current areas for play. Then spend approximately 15 minutes asking staff to look through their intended planning for the next half-term or organised topic. (This should be a future block of work in order that you will be able to develop ideas and resources in time for use.)
➤ Discuss and agree what the new areas will be and write these on to the plan clearly. For example, the role-play area could be a garage or airport; home play may remain initially as a general title.
➤ Now ask the staff to look at the more general titled areas and encourage them to discuss in pairs how these areas could be more tightly linked to overall topics, feeding back ideas for developing the play aspects.
➤ Give the example of a topic on 'Holidays' or 'Journeys'. The role-play area could be an airport with check-ins, passport control, hostessess and stewards, a plane interior and so on. The home play area could be enhanced with different bags and suitcases, choices of different clothing and items to pack, maps, brochures and so on. The construction area could be developed to require the children to build a hotel bedroom (or campsite) for your setting's toys on holiday. The outdoor play could be linked to an airport with parking zones, trolleys, arriving and departing visitors, taxis, buses and cars. Sand play could focus on beaches and holiday villages; water play on blue seas, various sealife, boats and swimmers!

➤ Give each member of staff a copy of the photocopiable sheets and ask them to work in pairs, or small groups, depending on your numbers. Allocate each small group a specific area from the plan. Invite the staff to move to this area and explore all their ideas for developing the play aspects related to your overall theme. Encourage them to complete the photocopiable sheets with their ideas. Spend approximately 15 minutes on this activity.

➤ Bring the whole group together and ask the staff to feed back ideas to each other for approximately 15 minutes. Allow all the staff to suggest further ideas where these extend learning by building on pairs' feedback.

➤ Agree what will be planned and give each pair one of the A4 cards and the red and blue pens.

➤ For the remaining time, ask the staff to title their card with the final choice of play activity for their allocated area. For example, 'Sand play – a tropical island setting'. Then encourage them to write beneath this what resources and equipment will be needed, itemising what is already available in blue, and what will need to be made or collected, in red. Let each group feed back to the others and see if staff can offer to provide equipment, artefacts or costumes.

➤ Add volunteers' names to the cards, or ideas for developing resources, such as 'Parents to be asked to send in buckets, spades and beach items' or 'Sewing group to make air stewards' tabards'.

➤ Invite the staff to take an empty storage box and label it to match their card. Put all the completed cards inside the appropriate boxes as a check-list for adding the resources ready for use.

Further action

➤ Allocate responsibility for overseeing each box to named staff members. Send letters home, informing parents of your plans and requesting their help with particular resources, or in making costumes and so on. Have the boxes handy in an appropriate area for the staff responsible to keep an eye on things and to alter check-lists accordingly as suitable resources are added.

➤ Plan a further session for the staff to come together to review resources and prepare further materials. Let them make labels, signs and notices which will extend learning in Communication, language and literacy or other Areas of Learning, for example, globes and maps. Identify related activities that could be undertaken to support the play activities and decide how these can be included in the teaching programme. This could be making their own passports with real photos or drawings, making foreign currency or designing a sun-hat. Also add cards prepared with key vocabulary and questions to the box, for the staff and helpers to use in order to bring a tight focus to learning.

Directed and independent work

Look at ways to give children a balance of directed and independent work

Number of staff
All.

Timing
45 minutes to 1 hour (depending on the number of staff involved).

What you need
A copy of the photocopiable sheet on page 133 for each member of staff; red and blue pens; A4 cards; glue (or a laminator); felt-tipped pens; flipchart; copy of the *Curriculum Guidance for the Foundation Stage* (available from QCA publications; tel: 01787 884444); current planning.

Preparation
➤ Copy these extracts from pages 15 and 16 of the QCA document on to the flipchart:
Principles for early years education
♦ 'Early years' experience should build on what children already know and can do.'
♦ 'Well-planned, purposeful activity and appropriate intervention by practitioners will engage children in the learning process.'
♦ 'To be effective, an early years curriculum should be carefully structured.'
♦ 'There should be opportunities for children to engage in activities planned by adults and also those that they plan or initiate themselves.'

What you do
➤ Explain that the aim of the session is to ensure that your setting gives children a balance of directed and independent work.
➤ Make a strong statement about the importance of this balance, highlighting the fact that frequently, OFSTED inspections judge that this balance is lacking in settings. Sometimes this is because of too little direction and adult interaction, in others cases it is because activities are so tightly directed that opportunities for the children to make choices or initiate their own ideas become too limited.
➤ Explain that the quotations from the flipchart are taken from the QCA publication, which includes the Early Learning Goals and Stepping Stones, and present it for reference for later activities. Take five minutes to read through the prepared flipchart and discuss each point, asking the staff to give an example, where possible, of an area of their recent work that would support each principle.
➤ Now ask the staff to work in pairs or small groups (depending on the size of your setting). Distribute red and blue pens to each group.
➤ Invite the pairs or small groups to go through their current week's planning carefully, putting a blue dot against directed activities and a red dot against opportunities for the children to initiate their own activities, or follow their own choices and ideas. Let the staff spend approximately ten minutes on this activity.
➤ Next, take approximately ten minutes to invite the pairs to feed back to the rest of the staff on what they have discovered. First, look at the overall balance and ask whether or not it is acceptable. The balance does not have to be exact, but should ensure that enough activities of both kinds exist.
➤ Then, for another ten minutes, ask the staff to select, and describe in detail, examples from their planning of both kinds of activity.

➤ Invite the staff to explain how:
♦ these are *directed* to build on previous learning
♦ what *adult intervention* will take place
♦ exactly how the children will be able to *initiate activities independently.*

➤ Allow time for the staff to discuss the examples and encourage them to ask questions of the presenting pairs.

➤ Give out the copies of the photocopiable sheet and briefly read through the headings.

➤ Now ask the staff to work in different pairs or groups, if staff numbers allow for this. For the remaining time, ask the new pairs first to go through their next week's planning, repeating the red and blue pen identification of where the different types of activity could take place within your setting.

➤ Then, let invite the staff to choose one red and one blue activity. Now encourage them to discuss how these will be implemented. Ask them to complete just one of their photocopiable sheets together, so as to give them a detailed planning 'aide memoire' to use when the activity is undertaken. (Retain the other photocopiable sheet for the staff to produce a final copy after feedback.)

➤ Encourage the pairs to feed back ideas to the whole group and ask all the staff to add their suggestions and ideas. Let each pair make a final, neat copy on the other photocopiable sheet, incorporating the agreed ideas for each activity that they discussed.

➤ Glue the photocopiable sheets to pieces of card, or laminate them, cutting them in half to provide the 'planning prompt' to accompany each chosen activity as it is undertaken the following week.

Further action

➤ Ask the staff to do the 'red and blue pen' analysis on a regular weekly basis and note the relative balance of activities. Where the balance is not quite right, ask them to ensure that subsequent planning addresses this. First, aim to have a good balance over time, with some of each activity clearly evident over the course of the week. As staff confidence grows, aim to plan these experiences on a daily basis, or at least several times a week.

➤ Keep the 'red and blue' system in place and use the marked planning (with a clear explanation of the codes!) as evidence for inspectors of your self-evaluation.

➤ Repeat the exercise using the photocopiable sheets regularly and build up a bank of good-quality 'planning prompt' cards that can be used repeatedly. These can be placed alongside each activity or given to those adults that may be involved in the organisation of the session. These will be particularly useful to guide support staff, students, parents and helpers.

➤ When working with parents and sharing information about the early years' curriculum, be sure to highlight the range of activities that you will provide and explain the need to have both directed and independent experiences. Make suggestions as to how parents and carers might also be involved in these at home.

Displays with impact

Consider how to create impressive displays to leave lasting impressions

⚞ Number of staff
All.

⏱ Timing
I hour 15 minutes (this could be divided into two sessions, if desired).

What you need
A copy of the photocopiable sheet on page 134 for each member of staff; six large sheets of paper (each titled with a different Early Learning Goal); flipchart or similar; felt-tipped pens; overhead projector (if possible); large sheet of pale-coloured sugar paper; examples of the children's drawings or writing; books/materials about the display subject.

Preparation
➤ Identify from your future planning, a large display that will be undertaken by your setting (something seasonal or the record of an event that everyone will be involved in would be best).
➤ Prepare a flipchart with the following:
The main purposes of display:
♦ to create a stimulating and inviting environment, with a high level of visual impact
♦ to reinforce learning
♦ to build on and extend learning
♦ to celebrate good work with children and build self-esteem and pride
♦ to celebrate good work with parents and visitors
♦ to set high standards in a highly visible manner.
➤ Leave space at the bottom for staff suggestions.

What you do
➤ Explain to the staff that the aim of this session is to help them focus on how they can maximise the children's learning through the provision of high-impact displays.
➤ Emphasise the fact that because such a lot of energy and time are invested in creating displays, the impact on learning should be worthwhile.
➤ Take five minutes to read through the chart, discussing the main purposes of the display. Ask the staff if they can think of any other purposes and, if so, add these to the bottom of the list.
➤ Now give each member of staff a photocopiable sheet. Spend a few minutes reading through the questions below, focusing on what evidence the staff would look for to help them make a judgement (these questions are expansions of those found on the photocopiable sheet, and have been phrased to encourage discussion):
♦ Do displays extend learning enough or are they too focused on decoration? Do they celebrate good work for children of different abilities?
♦ Have they involved the children enough?
♦ Is the balance of staff work too much?
♦ Do displays represent a wide range of the different Areas of Learning?
♦ Are there an appropriate range of titles, headings and questions to extend learning?
♦ Do displays provide opportunities to extend language and mathematical thinking?
♦ Is there a strong enough multicultural dimension to displays?
➤ Ask the staff to move around and look at all the displays around the setting, asking themselves these questions and jotting down their

views on the photocopiable sheet. You will need approximately 15 minutes for this task.

➤ Next, gather all the staff together and discuss your findings for another ten minutes, identifying those displays that have the most impact on learning, giving the reasons why. Also, identify ways that current displays could be made to have more impact by adjusting them, adding headings, signs and items – or even taking away some aspects that detract from learning!

➤ Share the title of a forthcoming topic or scheduled display of work. Show the group the reference books and materials that you have gathered and say that these are available for the staff to use.

➤ Divide the staff into pairs or small groups and give each pair a photocopiable sheet adding an Early Learning Goal as a heading.

➤ Ask them to discuss together and browse through the reference resources, writing down on the back of the photocopiable sheet their suggestions for productive displays – linked to the topic – that support their given Area of Learning. Suggest that they jot down ideas for questions, labels and so on that will extend the children's learning. Allow approximately ten minutes for this.

➤ Gather the group together and then spend another twenty minutes for each pair to feed back their ideas to everyone. As each pair complete their presentation, ask all the staff to suggest further ideas for extending learning or linking with their allocated Area of Learning. Make a point of stressing that the best displays can incorporate work from a wide range of different activities and related work.

➤ Make a note of all the best ideas so that you and all the staff will use

this information and plan this into the actual display in due course.

➤ Finally, explain that the use of children's own work is generally a major element of effective displays, although often their work may be small.

➤ Demonstrate to the staff how to enlarge a child's drawing by putting it on an overhead projector and drawing around the shape that is thrown on to a very large sheet of paper pinned to the wall. The child can then paint, colour or use collage to complete it for a display – the scale can make a very powerful impact indeed.

Further action

➤ Share with the staff the technique of using other examples of the children's work in a way that gives high impact. The children's writing or detailed drawings can also be enlarged by placing an acetate sheet over the top of it and copying carefully over the writing or picture with a dark transparency pen. Then project the work on to large sheets of paper, and ink in the image. The children and parents are usually amazed and delighted by the results!

➤ Arrange time for a further staff-training session to let them try this using current work, ready for their own displays, signs and notices, class big books and so on.

Outdoor learning

Look at ways to maximise the quality of your outdoor learning programme

⅍ Number of staff
All.

🕐 Timing
I hour.

What you need
A copy of photocopiable sheet on page 135 for each member of staff; the *Curriculum Guidance for the Foundation Stage* (QCA) (available from QCA Publications, tel: 01787 884444); pens; scissors; sticky tape; large-scale plan of your setting including all outdoor areas; coloured felt-tipped pens; flipchart.

Preparation
➤ Draw a very large-scale sketch map of your setting, clearly showing the building with pathways, exits and entrances and all of its surrounding areas. Use colour to indicate grass, soft-play and hard-play areas. Mark in fixed apparatus or permanent items (canopies, wall-mounted blackboards and so on).
➤ Prepare the flipchart with the following statements taken from page 102 of the QCA publication:
Physical development
Teaching
'The role of the practitioner is crucial in planning and providing an environment that encourages children to do things, talk about what they are doing and think about how they can improve their actions or movements.
    '...effective teaching requires:
♦ providing opportunities for regular and frequent physical activity indoors and outdoors
♦ ensuring that space is safe to use, and that outdoor clothing is safe and sensible'.
➤ Prepare another sheet with the heading:
Developments and resources.

What you do
➤ Explain that the aim of this session is to review and develop the quality and range of your outdoor learning programme, within a safe environment.
➤ Refer to the flipchart and the extracts, drawing the staff's attention to the fact that, although these points are quoted from the Physical development Area of Learning, outdoor activities should support learning in every other area. Spend approximately five minutes encouraging the staff to describe examples of activities from their current practice and how these help the children learn across other Areas of Learning.
➤ Take another five minutes or so to make a strong statement that all outdoor activities need to have a focus. Outdoor 'free-playtime', without a well thought-out purpose (or used as a general break for the staff and the children!) wastes valuable time for learning. Point out that this does not spoil opportunities for a spontaneous reaction to events, such as investigating a snowfall or to observe builders in action. Such spontaneous activities should also have a clear learning focus, even if only decided at the last minute!
➤ Also, stress that OFSTED inspectors frequently find that outdoor activities are too limited and that they lack challenge and stimulation, or that adults do not interact sufficiently. For example, it is not sufficient to simply 'patrol' play areas. It is better to become involved

and move the children's learning on, through appropriate intervention.

➤ Spend a few minutes pointing out the features on your plan to remind the staff of the available environment. Mention that the children see all the areas and can be influenced by their impact, although some zones are not accessible to them. Mark any areas that the children must not venture into for safety reasons. Identify everywhere that the children could visit with proper supervision.

➤ Give each member of staff a copy of the photocopiable sheet and ask them to work in pairs. Go through the headings together and explain that they are to go around all the available outdoor areas together. Encourage them to think creatively with new ideas or improvements to old ones! Ask them to complete the petals on the sheet, cut them out and tape them to the appropriate place on the large-scale plan of the setting.

➤ Display the prepared chart titled 'Developments and resources'. Explain that where the staff suggest new developments, such as 'reorganise group times for smaller group outdoor activities' or 'raise funds for picnic tables' and so on, they should write these on the chart. Allow 30 minutes for this task.

➤ For the remaining time, gather the whole staff together and share all the ideas for the different areas. Encourage the staff to build on the initial suggestions in more detail. Write on the plan those activities that will form part of your provision. Bear in mind that you can have a whole range of activities for different areas that can be covered over a period of time! Try to ensure that there is a good, varied range that will enable the staff to ring the changes and keep activities fresh.

➤ Consider the list of suggestions and decide together how these might be tackled. Agree those that can be implemented and elect a lead staff member to organise actions or further research.

➤ For simple suggestions, such as new play-area markings, organise a working group to carry out the tasks as soon as possible.

➤ Choose the dates for introducing changes or, if appropriate, discussing new arrangements further.

➤ Decide the priority order for obtaining new resources and put the agreed number against the items. This will give you an agreed 'shopping list' for when the money becomes available or give you a focus for any fund-raising projects.

Further action

➤ Carry out this activity on a seasonal basis. Focus on how outdoor activities can still be undertaken in inclement or winter weather. For example, a setting could gather a set of cagoules and wellingtons so that the children can be properly clothed for brief outdoor excursions. Consider how and where gardening, sand, water play and construction activities could be organised in the summer months.

➤ Organise visits to other settings to investigate how they use their environments, or discuss this with teacher-mentors or local education authority support staff.

Using the locality productively

Focus on taking full advantage of your local environment

Number of staff
All.

Timing
45 minutes.

What you need
The *Curriculum Guidance for the Foundation Stage* (QCA) (available from QCA publications, tel: 01787 884444); flipchart; felt-tipped pens; local map; paper; pens; local telephone directory; Yellow Pages; large sheets of paper; Post-it notes or similar; copies of your planning.

Preparation
➤ On the flipchart, copy out these Early Learning Goals taken from the Knowledge and understanding of the world Area of Learning in the *Curriculum Guidance for the Foundation Stage* (QCA):
'Look closely at similarities, differences, patterns and change'.
'Ask questions about why things happen and how things work'.
'Find out about past and present events in their own lives, and in those of their families and other people they know'.
'Observe, find out about and identify features in the place they live and the natural world'.
'Find out about their environment, and talk about those features they like and dislike'.
'Begin to know about their own cultures and beliefs and those of other people'.
➤ On another sheet of the flipchart, make a list of all the areas of the locality that your setting currently uses such as shops, park, churches and so on.
➤ On each of the large sheets of paper, write one title per sheet, of each forthcoming topic or theme that your setting is likely to follow during the coming year – long-term projects. such as 'Autumn', 'Journeys' and so on, and also the short-term ones for special festivals, such as Pancake Day.

What you do
➤ Explain that the aim of this session is to consider how your setting can develop its use of the local environment to extend the children's learning effectively.
➤ Make a positive statement emphasising that using the local environment can greatly support the children's learning in Knowledge and understanding of the world. Display the flipchart with the Early Learning Goals extracts. Spend five minutes reading through the extracts and ask the staff to suggest examples of where their current use of the environment supports learning in these Goals. Write these on the chart in coloured felt-tipped pen. In a contrasting coloured pen, also note any areas that current practice does not support quite so well.
➤ Remind the staff that many other Areas of Learning can also be supported by using the local environment extensively. Give the staff five minutes to make a list of some activities that could be followed through using the local environment more. Ask them to think of examples for every Area of Learning. Spend another five minutes letting staff feed back their ideas.
➤ Now reveal the list of the current environment use and run through it quickly, adding any other uses that the staff remember. Discuss how useful these environmental links have been and what learning benefits have resulted. Try to identify any environmental resources that have not yet been used.

Ask the staff:

♦ Do we use shops and supermarkets? What do we do there? What different use could we make of the visits there?

♦ Have we visited fire stations, the veterinary surgery, medical centres and so on?

♦ Do we visit the local library? How does this extend the children's learning? How could we make more of the library?

♦ Have we visited the local churches and religious centres? What have we done there? How might this be developed?

♦ Have we planned 'street trails' to look at new and old houses, different building materials, gardens and street furniture?

♦ Have we looked at different physical features such as hills, bends, busy roads, quiet lanes, parks; open spaces, built-up areas and so on.

♦ Have we visited parks and contrasted what we see in different seasons? Have we looked at play areas and other public facilities?

♦ Are there any clubs and societies in our area that we could link with? Where else might we go?

➤ Ask the staff to work in pairs or small groups, depending on the size of your setting. Make the local map and the telephone directories available for reference. Give each pair a sheet with a topic title. If you are a small setting, you may need to repeat this activity to cover all the topic titles.

➤ Ask the staff to use the local maps and reference material, as well as knowledge of the locality and your outdoor setting, to think of possible visits or links that could be explored in order to enrich learning in each topic. Invite them to list these ideas on the sheets. Spend approximately 20 minutes on this activity.

➤ Come back together for ten minutes, with each pair presenting their suggestions to the others and highlighting the Areas of Learning that would be enhanced. Let everyone contribute their own ideas to the initial suggestions. Agree together the most interesting ones to pursue and write the places down on Post-it notes.

➤ Share out the Post-it notes among the staff and ask each member to make a visit to their suggested venue, or to follow up the idea by exploring the feasibility of links. Agree a date by which this will be done and have another session to decide how new arrangements can be built into your planning.

Further action
➤ Set up a file of local contacts and information from staff research to keep for future reference and use, so that you can build visits into your programme in due course.
➤ Contact local art galleries and museums to see if visits can be arranged, and find out if any transport grants are available.

A check-list for your setting concerning the issues raised in **Chapter 3** Maximising resources and the environment

➤ Do you regularly and systematically review your existing resources? How is this done?

➤ Do you ensure that damaged materials are updated and repaired? How is this done?

➤ Do you discard damaged and worn out equipment or leave it to clutter up storerooms?

➤ Do you have regular reviews of any outdoor environment resources (climbing frames, gardens, playground markings and so on)?

➤ Do you have a running list of what resources you will need to purchase when money allows?

➤ Have you got a priority list of necessary resources and does your budget and spending reflect these needs?

➤ Have you checked through your planning to ensure that you have the correct resources for the programme you intend?

➤ Are the staff given responsibility and opportunities to develop resources matched to planning?

➤ Have you reviewed the quality of play activities that your setting offers? What are the strengths and weaknesses?

➤ How can weaknesses be overcome?

➤ Are parents, helpers and the community approached for help in providing – or making – appropriate resources to extend play and other areas of the children's learning?

➤ Are you developing 'resource boxes' that can be used to support specific planned home play or similar activities?

➤ How could you review the balance of directed and independent activities and ensure that this is maintained or improved?

➤ How might you track individual children's choices to ensure that they have a balanced experience?

➤ How do you help the staff to become sensitively skilled in adult intervention?

➤ What is the quality and balance of your display?

➤ Is the majority of any display the children's own work, or is there too much adult input?

➤ Are there sufficient literacy and numeracy headings, questions and references?

➤ Does any Area of Learning receive too little display? If so, how could this be addressed?

➤ Have you walked around your setting at child's height to get a child's eye view of your environment?

➤ What types of outdoor play do you provide?

➤ How do you ensure that outdoor play is still covered in the winter months or poor weather?

➤ How is outdoor play planned for?

➤ What opportunities are there to develop different kinds of outdoor play in your setting?

➤ What further resources would you need to keep outdoor play fresh and stimulating?

➤ What opportunities and facilities present themselves in your setting's locality?

➤ How many of these do you exploit?

➤ How might you find out more about local facilities that your setting could be involved with?

➤ How could more use be made of the local environment to extend the children's learning?

Chapter 4 Working with parents and the community

There are rich benefits to be gained from parents and early years practitioners supporting each other in extending children's learning. This chapter will help you to develop these vital links.
Good settings have always worked hard to develop productive relationships with parents. It is useful for all settings to consider the quality of their existing parental partnerships and seek ways to strengthen this further.

Parents' views
OFSTED inspections give a great emphasis to parents' views and the way that the setting actively endeavours to involve parents in their children's learning. This is further endorsed throughout the *Curriculum Guidance for the Foundation Stage* (QCA).

The first activity on page 52 is designed as a training session for staff to review their own practice and consider a range of good practice ideas for involving parents further. The unit is closely linked to the expectations laid down by the QCA.

This is further developed in the activity on page 54 where the issue of good communication is explored. Good communications are often taken for granted and this unit gives early years settings a chance to review what they do and gives suggestions for extending it. Your own practice is the starting-point and staff will work together to consider how to draw an annual calendar of effective and varied ways to build on your current systems.

Home learning
In early years education today, there is an increasing emphasis placed on the role of home learning and how parents can play an active part in extending their children's learning. The activity on page 56 will be a starting-point for all the staff to contribute ideas to improve your own practice in this area, and should lead on to producing materials and resources that parents can use at home to complement your own programmes in your setting.

The activity on page 58 focuses on parents working alongside the children in the setting. This training unit is aimed at enabling staff to strengthen parental working relationships within a setting and to ensure that their contribution is as effective as possible.

Visitors
All good settings are keen to let their children have a wide range of experiences, including meeting visitors at the setting. The activity on page 60 is planned to enable all the staff to look at developing this important area and maximising the impact that visitors can make on learning. The link between your own planned themes and programmes is also stressed so that visitors become an integral part of your provision.

Finally, the activity on page 62 gives the staff an opportunity to reflect on the potential – and often untapped – resources that are readily available within their local community. It gives a bank of ideas for staff to use to develop better links to benefit your setting.

Developing parental partnerships

Concentrate on establishing positive relationships with parents

♞ Number of staff
All.

◷ Timing
45 minutes.

What you need
A copy of photocopiable sheet on page 136 for each member of staff; pens; paper; flipchart; felt-tipped pens; the *Curriculum Guidance for the Foundation Stage* (QCA) (available from QCA Publications, tel: 01787 884444).

What you do
➤ Explain that the aim of the session is to look at how your setting actively seeks to establish positive partnerships with parents and to develop these further.
➤ Show the staff the statements prepared on your first sheet on the flipchart. Read through the first two statements and ask the staff to suggest examples of why these assertions are valid. Write the staffs' comments in the spaces and discuss them for approximately five minutes.
➤ Draw the staff's attention to the final statement and make a strong affirmation of its importance in your setting. Reveal the second sheet and explain that there is not one correct

Preparation
➤ Use the flipchart to write out the following extracts from pages 9 and 10 of the *Curriculum Guidance for the Foundation Stage* (QCA).
➤ On the first sheet of paper, leave a space between each of the first two statements and write:
Parents as partners
♦ Parents are the children's first and most enduring educators.
♦ When parents and practitioners work together in early years settings, the results have a positive impact on the child's development and learning.
♦ Therefore, each setting should seek to develop an effective partnership with parents.'
➤ On the second sheet of paper, write:
'There are many ways of achieving partnerships with parents...'.
➤ Write each one of the following titles on a separate sheet of paper:

1 Practitioners show respect for the role of parents in their children's education.
2 The past and future roles of parents in the education of children is recognised and actively encouraged.
3 Practitioners listen carefully to parents' views about their child and their concerns.
4 Flexible arrangements support parents and practitioners talking together about their children.
5 Parents are made to feel welcome and valued.
6 The expertise of parents (and the wider family) is used to support learning.
7 Practitioners use a variety of ways to inform parents about the curriculum.
8 Parents and practitioners share and record information about children together.
9 Home links and activities are actively encouraged.

way of establishing productive partnerships. Each setting should develop their own ideas based on their unique situation.

➤ Reveal the other nine sheets of paper, one by one, and read through the headings, explaining that these are based on the guidance in the QCA document. Take approximately five minutes to share these together.

➤ Divide the staff into pairs or small groups. Display the first sheet and look at the heading together. Ask them to say what already happens in your setting and give examples of your usual practice. For example, 'Parents are asked to send in a photograph of their child for a display.' Write comments on the sheet using a brightly coloured felt-tipped pen.

➤ Then ask them to suggest what *could* happen, or ideas for developing links even more, such as 'Use the photos to go in a joint parents'/practitioners' record file for each child.' Write these on the chart in a contrasting colour.

➤ Give each pair at least two of the other titled sheets and two different coloured felt-tipped pens. Explain that they will have approximately 15 minutes to consider each title and then complete the sheet.

➤ Gather the group together and display their sheets around the room for everyone to see. Spend approximately ten minutes sharing and discussing their contributions.

➤ Give a copy of the photocopiable sheet to each person and ask them to work once more in pairs or small groups. Briefly, read through the headings together. Ask the staff to refer to the 'Good ideas bank', plus the group sheets around the room, discussing possible ideas. Then ask them to complete the 'In our setting we could...' section. Take approximately 15 minutes for this.

➤ Gather the staff together once more and feed back staff ideas.

➤ Agree two ideas to be introduced first and decide when and how these will be launched. Also decide who will lead the development.

Our photographs

Further action

➤ Collate the most workable ideas for extending productive partnerships and organise these into priority order. Look at the highest priority proposals first and allocate a start date, preparation time-scale and implementation deadline. Plan how you will introduce the new developments.

➤ Ensure that those you give high priority to will have maximum impact, but choose a balance of easy-to-implement and longer-term developments on your list. For example, developing a bank of games and activities, bagged up with prepared instructions and ready for home loan, might be a high priority to involve parents more out of your setting. However, this will take time to gather and prepare all the necessary resources and so the introduction date will need to reflect this. Asking parents to feed information into a joint record could have a much earlier introduction, once all the staff are clear how the process will take place.

Good communications

Focus on building alliances with parents and outside agencies

👪 Number of staff
All.

🕐 Timing
Approximately 45 minutes.

What you need
A copy of the photocopiable sheet on page 137 for each member of staff; pens; flipchart; red and blue felt-tipped pens; the *Curriculum Guidance for the Foundation Stage* (QCA) (available from QCA Publications, tel: 01787 884444); your setting's induction programme; parents' information booklets; general communications with parents; parents' meeting dates; dates of meetings with feeder schools.

Preparation
➤ On the flipchart, write out the following extract from the *Curriculum Guidance for the Foundation Stage* (QCA) (taken from page 9), leaving a space between each principle:

'Parents as partners

♦ 'A successful partnership needs a two-way flow of information, knowledge and expertise.'

♦ 'All parents are made to feel welcome, valued and necessary through a range of different opportunities for collaboration between children, parents and practitioners.'

♦ 'Practitioners use a variety of ways to keep parents fully informed about the curriculum, such as brochures, displays and videos which are available in the home language of the parents, and through informal discussion.'

➤ On another sheet of paper, write the heading 'Calendar of communications' and divide the rest of the space into a grid of 12 equal squares, labelling each one with a month of the year.

What you do
➤ Explain that the aim of this session is to ensure that your setting's communication with parents, and other relevant agencies, is positive and productive.

➤ Reveal the flipchart headings taken from the *Curriculum Guidance for the Foundation Stage* (QCA). Read through the extracts together and make a strong affirmation statement that your setting's philosophy supports these principles.

➤ Take approximately ten minutes to go through the extracts again. This time, ask the staff to put forward the practical ways that they currently work and communicate with parents that show evidence of this support. Write these on the chart in a contrasting felt-tipped pen.

➤ Make a note on a separate sheet of any areas that your setting currently does not use, or only partly uses. Keep these for later reference.

➤ Now distribute a copy of the photocopiable sheet to each person and read through the headings together. Explain that the staff will shortly look at the current information samples and arrangements for communication with parents for your setting, using the photocopiable checklist.

➤ Let the staff work in pairs to complete the sheets, reviewing current practice and suggesting ways to improve it. Spend approximately 15 minutes on this activity.

➤ Gather the staff together and let pairs feed back on their views and suggestions. Refer back to the photocopiable sheets, discussing areas that your setting does not yet fully implement. Take approximately ten minutes for this task.

➤ Ask the staff to consider which ideas and improvements you could make. Make a note of any agreed ideas on a large sheet of paper.

➤ Finally, introduce the calendar chart. Spend the remaining time writing in your current agreed good practice, plus when any of the new ideas could be incorporated. For example, 'September – Developing a new setting style for parents' letters, using a unique character'; 'January – Introducing a monthly parents' newsletter with illustrations of the children's work and photographs', 'February – Developing a system to inform parents of our curriculum topics' and 'May – Introducing this system'. Add these in blue pen.

➤ Ensure that the communications are spaced out well over the year and that certain periods are not overloaded. Make any adjustments necessary and go through the months filling in names of the staff who will lead developments in the different areas.

➤ Make sure that all the staff know of any further tasks they will take on and when these need to be ready for further staff discussions.

➤ Also make a note of any resource implications and how these will be resolved, such as:

◆ increasing suitable paper stock for newsletters in a chosen colour (from general budget)

◆ setting aside time and materials to design a new special setting cover for information packs (staff release and staff meetings)

◆ setting up a Parents' noticeboard (seek parents' help and materials, school PTA request)

◆ buying or borrowing a digital camera for action photos of your setting at work (fund-raising drive, initially requesting help from parents)

◆ getting a video and making a video of aspects of your work (staff loan)

◆ if appropriate, time to liaise with ethnic-minority community leaders and to arrange mother-tongue translations of texts and video 'voice-overs'. (Local consultation is important as many ethnic minority communities prefer text communications in English as parents may prefer to ask their bilingual friends to translate for them.) (Manager time.)

◆ use of a scanner for including children's work in information (liaise with local school to seek use of facilities)

◆ computer time, perhaps even designing a setting website! (Consult main school or parents.)

Further action

➤ Try to develop a 'house style' for all your communications. Choosing a particular and bright colour for all newsletters and communications ensures that parents and carers really notice them! Selecting a setting 'character' (such as an animal or toy) and using this to decorate all newsletters and communications, raises the profile of your information and is attractive to the children. This specific character 'logo' can also be used to really good effect on noticeboards and signs all around the setting.

Developing home learning ideas

Consider how to involve parents in their children's learning

♦♦♦ Number of staff
All.

⏱ Timing
Approximately 1 hour.

What you need
A4 card; pens; Post-it notes or similar; flipchart; felt-tipped pens; collection of your setting's home-learning materials; any examples loaned from other settings; drawstring bag (approximately 30cm x 30cm) plastic A4 wallet for each person; the *Curriculum Guidance for the Foundation Stage* (QCA) (available from QCA Publications, tel: 01787 884444).

Preparation
➤ Contact other settings and arrange a visit to see what home learning packs and materials they use, or contact your local teacher-mentor for information and the loan of any materials.
➤ Make a drawstring bag from brightly coloured fabric remnants (curtains from charity shops are ideal!) for each member of staff.
➤ On one of the large sheets of paper, copy out this extract from pages 9 and 10 of the QCA document: 'Parents as partners'
'There are many ways of achieving partnership with parents, but the following are common features of effective practice:
...relevant learning activities and play activities, such as reading and sharing books, are continued at home. Similarly, experiences at home are used to develop learning in the setting, for example visits and celebrations.'

What you do
➤ Explain that the aim of this session is to consider how to develop effective home links with parents that extend children's learning.
➤ Look at the QCA publication extract and discuss it together. Make a positive statement about the benefits to children of *both* areas of home learning. Explain that this session is concerned with developing ideas for extending learning at home and involving parents in the process.
➤ Display your home learning materials, plus any others that you have borrowed, and spend approximately ten minutes looking at these together. If you have few resources to discuss, move on to the next activity.
➤ Spend approximately ten minutes going through the check-list below as some starter suggestions of ideas that are commonly used in early years settings to promote parental involvement and extend children's learning at home.

Check-list
♦ Parents come into the setting at a fixed time/date and help their children to choose and change books from a 'home learning book box'.
♦ 'Story sacks' are created with one book plus a card of ideas for parents to use related to the reading activity.
♦ Staff set up a 'home loan' set of large toys and construction equipment (in plastic carrying boxes) for weekend and holiday borrowing – this can be booked by parents or directed/ encouraged for individuals by staff.

♦ 'Maths magic' kits are created containing dice, sorting and counting equipment and so on, plus cards with games instructions for parents.

♦ Topic packs, related to current curriculum studies, are developed. These may contain resources, such as pictures to talk about, books, maps and artefacts, plus ideas cards with suggested activities, for example, 'Go for a walk and notice all the different vehicles that you see. Help your child to make a list of these next to his or her drawings'.

♦ Wallets containing task sheets and a range of resources such as scissors, shapes for cutting out, glue sticks, threading and safe sewing materials, colouring pencils or crayons, sticky shapes and so on.

♦ 'Bulky packs' containing paint, paper and brushes, glue and collage scraps and so on, with ideas cards.

♦ Specific soft toys, perhaps related to your setting's character logo, such as 'Rainbow Ted', and a large diary. The toys are sent home, or on holiday with the family, and parents are asked to help their child fill in the diary with words and pictures and stuck-in tickets to show what Ted did with the family.

♦ 'Away packs' of ideas for activities while the child is on holiday or absent, such as a plain postcard for the child to illustrate and send to you, card jigsaws or simple games to play with parents.

➤ On the second sheet of paper, write a title: 'Ideas for home-learning materials'. Give each person two or three Post-it notes. Ask the staff to work in pairs and use these to record their suggestions for home-learning ideas that could work for your setting. Ask them to add them to your 'Ideas' sheet. Take ten minutes for this task.

➤ Take a further ten minutes to share everyone's ideas and discuss how these could be practically developed. Agree which ideas you will put into practice.

➤ With a flourish, produce your drawstring bags, wallets and the A4 card and give these out to everyone! For the remaining time, ask the staff to choose which agreed ideas they will adopt and ask them to begin to prepare these for the receptacles. Ask them to plan out the parents' instructions on the cards.

➤ Give out more Post-it notes and ask staff to write down their activity titles and make a list of the materials which they will need to put into their packs. Make a note of any resources that you will need to obtain.

➤ Plan some time to complete the packs and share them with colleagues.

Further action
➤ Work out how and when the new packs will be introduced to parents. If you have a small staff it will take time to produce enough packs for every family to use, so you may need to set a target of producing these over a term. Consider setting up a parents' group to help with the task, making resources, laminating instructions and so on.

Parents working in the setting

Concentrate on strengthening effective relationships with parents

ᨁ Number of staff
All.

⏱ Timing
Approximately 45 minutes.

What you need
A copy of photocopiable sheet on page 138 for each member of staff; paper; pens; copies of your current planning; flipchart; felt-tipped pens.

Preparation
➤ Prepare the flipchart with the following title and questions, leaving a large enough space for the answers to be added:

Parents working in our setting

♦ Do we make parents and carers welcome?
♦ How?
♦ How do we know that we do?
♦ Do we have parents in the setting during their children's induction?
♦ What do they actually do?
♦ What do we expect them to do?
♦ How many parents do we have working with us?
♦ Should we have more or less?
♦ If we have too few, why is this?
♦ Do we have men and women?
♦ How do we seek to attract them in?
♦ How do we seek to retain them?
♦ How do we approach parents, grandparents, carers and other potential adult helpers?
♦ What different strategies could we adopt?
♦ What roles do parents play?
♦ How useful are they?
♦ What more could they do?
♦ How do we support them?
♦ Do we do enough to help them help us?
♦ What more could we do?
♦ What are the benefits of having parents in our setting?
♦ Are there any problems having parents in?
♦ If so, how do we tackle these?

What you do
➤ Explain that the aim of this session is to consider how you can build and strengthen productive relationships with parents working within your setting.
➤ Reveal the flipchart and spend approximately 15 minutes asking the staff the questions and discussing their answers and related comments. Summarise the emerging views and write these under the matching questions.
➤ Read through the final answers and put a circle around any areas that require further action.
➤ Make a positive statement stressing that parents working in settings make a beneficial contribution to the children's learning when their roles are well managed. Stress that the important issue is that everyone – practitioners as well as the parents themselves – should know exactly what their role is during their visit.
➤ Now take five minutes to ask everyone to list all the recent occasions when parents have worked alongside other staff. List exactly what parent helpers were asked to do.
➤ Review the resulting list and spend another five minutes asking:
♦ How did parents know what to do?
♦ Did we make clear how they were to interact with the children?
♦ Did they know what we wanted the children to experience, to learn and to understand?
♦ Were they clear which questions to ask?
♦ Were they clear about the vocabulary that should be stressed?

◆ Do we have an easy and manageable system for informing parents before the activity and receiving feedback from them afterwards?

➤ Now ask the staff to refer to their plans for the following week and identify where any parents would be working with them at a particular time or on a specific activity. If parents are not due at that time, but are scheduled in for a particular future occasion or event, such as accompanying children on a visit, helping at a picnic or taking a group for cookery, select one of these as a focus. (If your setting has no parents at all helping in school, select a future planned activity where parental help may be valuable.)

➤ Give out the photocopiable sheets to each person. Spend a few minutes going through the headings and explain that the staff will use the sheet to prepare a 'Parent helper card' for a precise activity. Ask them to work in pairs, or small groups if numbers permit, taking it in turns to help each individual complete the sheet for their chosen activity. Allow 15 minutes for this task.

➤ Gather the group together. For most of the remaining time ask each person, in turn, to explain what their chosen activity was and then to share their completed sheets with the rest of the group. Encourage discussion and ask colleagues to consider whether, if they were the parent helpers, they would be clear about what to do and how best to help the children learn. Make any adjustments after discussion.

➤ For the last few minutes, return to the initial list of questions and the areas that were circled for further attention. Decide which of these needs to be the subject of another session and plan one into the diaries.

Further action

➤ Ask the staff to make copies of their completed sheets and then use them at the appropriate time. Ensure that they also ask parents to give their views about how helpful or otherwise the cards were!

➤ It would be useful to prepare a selection of 'Parent helper cards' to accompany a whole range of different activities. These could be made permanent by photocopying the sheet on to card and laminating it. Staff and parents could complete the appropriate sections using a dry-marker pen or china-graph pencil. These could be cleaned off easily after use and the cards used repeatedly.

➤ Send out a questionnaire to parents and carers to elicit those who would be interested in working in school regularly, occasionally or for special events. Seek out any personal interests or skills that you might ask them to share, such as cooking, sewing, music, gardening, art and craft, woodwork, animals, travelling and so on. Acknowledge all positive returns with an invitation and build up a register of potential helpers.

Maximising the impact of visitors

Consider how a range of visitors will have an effect on children's learning

👥 Number of staff
All.

🕐 Timing
Initially 1 hour plus follow-up time.

What you need
Copies of your long-term planning, with topics or themes identified for the year, if possible; flipchart; felt-tipped pens; paper; pens.

Preparation
➤ Go through your topic and theme titles, including special events and celebrations, such as Bonfire Night, Eid, Christmas and annual visits, and list each one as a title on a separate sheet of paper on the flipchart.

What you do
➤ Explain that the aim of this session is to consider the impact on learning of a range of different visitors, and seek ways to increase this in your setting.
➤ Write the heading 'Potential visitors' on the flipchart.
➤ Ask the staff to think of all the different visitors that could be invited into your setting and write these down on the chart. Take approximately ten minutes for this.
➤ Once the ideas are complete, check the list against the following check-list of visitors commonly associated with settings and see how yours compares:

Check-list
Nurse
Medical officer
Dentist
Firefighter
Road-safety team
Ambulance officer
Caretaker
Crossing-patrol person
Vicar
Priest
Religious leader
Museum curator
Local shopkeeper
Librarian
Police officer
Parent helpers
Grandparents
Adult 'Friends of your setting'
Students
Tutors
Teacher-mentors
Visiting staff
Governors
Managers
Local community representatives
Specialist interest visitors ('Animal Man' or artists)
Grounds maintenance staff
Builder
Health and safety official
Commercial representative.

➤ If there are any on the check-list that you have not thought of, consider whether these could be further investigated as possible extensions for your setting. If so, add these to your list. Keep the list displayed for reference.
➤ Reveal the first of your prepared topic title lists. Take approximately ten minutes to fill in, under the title, all the visitors who are already involved at your setting – and add, in brackets, what they will be doing.
➤ Look through your original 'Potential visitors' list to see if there could be any useful connections

early years
*training &
management*

there. For example, if you have a theme on 'Nursery rhymes' planned, consider whether a visit from a librarian might extend learning well. She or he may be able to bring a selection of books to share with the children. You could also hold an informal parents' workshop or coffee session at which the librarian could promote home reading and library services. Write down all the ideas for visitors and how they could work for the greatest impact on the children's learning.

➤ Now ask the staff to work in pairs or small groups. Share out the topic or theme title sheets that you prepared earlier.

➤ For the next 20 minutes, invite the staff to refer to any planning, and list any existing visitor arrangements. Then ask them to refer to your completed 'Potential visitor' list and fill in any further visitor links that would support the theme. State the sort of visitor and what they might be asked to do, or whether they should be contacted for ideas.

➤ Gather the staff back together and take approximately 15 minutes for each pair or group to feed back their ideas to the rest of the group.

➤ For the remaining time available, discuss all the suggestions and ask the group to decide which ideas will be followed up and adopted. Circle all the agreed ideas in a bright colour. Decide which staff will be responsible for making contact with the potential visitors and what arrangements will be made to follow up the staff requests and suggestions.

➤ After the session, let the staff follow up their assigned contact, investigate possibilities, set up the dates and report back to colleagues. Make sure that they ensure that their visitor knows all the

expectations of what they are to do during the visit and who they will be working with. Let allocated staff assume responsibility for welcoming the visitor, making any arrangements and organising the visit.

➤ Ensure that police clearance requirements are followed where visitors are to be working in a situation that deems it necessary. If in doubt, consult your local authority, teacher-mentor or manager.

Further action

➤ Prepare a brief but informative and attractive booklet to send in advance to all visitors. Make that sure it contains an outline of the unique elements of your setting including:
♦ the age range of your children
♦ the general facilities
♦ the general organisation (groups, key workers, integrated sessions and so on)
♦ the organisation of the day (times of sessions, special arrangements)
♦ health and safety issues (fire-alarm and evacuation instructions, child protection issues and supervision, out-of-bounds areas, non-smoking rules and so on)
♦ any other essential information for an occasional visitor (staffroom, toilets, parking and so on).

➤ In addition, have a page to be completed specifically for each different visitor, with the title:
 'We are delighted that you are coming to visit us!' followed by:
♦ date and start/finish times
♦ During your visit you will work with... (list the group or class).
♦ You are going to... (describe what agreed actions they will take or programme they will follow).
♦ These resources will be available for you... (list resources).
♦ ... (staff name) will be your host for your visit. Ask him or her for anything you need.
♦ Thank you for finding the time to visit us! We hope that you will enjoy working with us.

➤ Collect the booklets in after the visit and write in, as a record, any evaluation points to help you make any necessary future adjustments.

Fully exploiting community links

Explore ways for your setting to be an important part of the local community

👥 Number of staff
All.

⏱ Timing
45 minutes.

What you need
A copy of photocopiable sheet on page 139 for each person; pens; flipchart; felt-tipped pens; large map of the local area; lolly sticks; green and yellow sticky paper; scissors; Plasticine; your setting's headed notepaper; large envelopes; copies of your setting's brochure; local telephone directories; list of contacts for local organisations.

Preparation
➤ Visit your local library and ask for details of clubs, groups and organisations that meet locally.
➤ Look at posters in local shops to find contacts for potential community links (such as the artists' society, aquatic club, sports groups and so on).
➤ Write titles and contacts on the flipchart.
➤ Walk around the local environment and make a note of parks and interesting houses and gardens, different types of shops, companies and commercial operations. Investigate what some small local firms produce (it is not always obvious from outside!). Write your survey findings on the flipchart.
➤ Make a large lolly stick and sticky-paper flag with your setting's name on it.

What you do
➤ Explain that the aim of this session is twofold:
♦ to look at the potential of your local area and community and find ways to exploit the local richness and diversity for the benefit of your children's learning and your setting's development;

♦ to raise the profile of your setting within its local community.
➤ Also make a definitive statement that community links should be a two-way process and benefit all parties. Although extremely useful, community links are not just about attracting funds from local groups! An important element is for local firms and groups to know about your setting and to value it as part of their community, too.
➤ Stress that your local community will have many sources of stimulus for your children's learning. There are several potential visitors who could bring a new dimension to your setting. (It would be useful for your staff to carry out the activity 'Maximising the impact of visitors' on page 60, once these have been identified.)
➤ Reveal the local information on clubs and societies and talk about your survey findings for approximately five minutes. Draw your staff's attention to any interesting sites you discovered on your local survey. Inform them of the business of some local companies.
➤ Distribute the photocopiable sheets and ask the staff to work individually to complete the 'Community links' treasure chest'. Ask them to refer to the information that you have discovered and use their own local knowledge and the local telephone directory for ideas. Take ten minutes for this task.
➤ Lay out the local map on a large table. Mark your setting's position with the prepared lolly-stick flag. Ask the staff to compare their

'Community links' ideas and select the most useful and varied ones that will either extend the children's learning or help to raise your setting's profile in the community.

➤ Give pairs of staff lolly-sticks, scissors and sticky paper. Ask them to make green flags, with names of suitable local places with potential links to extend learning, and yellow flags where links might raise the setting's profile. Remember to include clubs and societies that meet locally. Fix these on to the map with Plasticine. Allow approximately 15 minutes for this activity.

➤ Spend approximately ten minutes reviewing what has been marked and deciding the most useful links to pursue.

➤ Together, compose a short letter on the flipchart, introducing your setting and giving some brief information about yourselves. Agree dates for the guests to be invited to your setting and what form this will take. It would be useful to have a rolling programme of dates to prevent guest overload!

➤ Below is an example of a letter that could be sent out to prospective visitors.

Rainbow Days Nursery Group

Dear

May we introduce ourselves? We are a small nursery group in your local community catering for *(number of)* children from ... years to ... years of age. Some of our children attend for half days and a few are full-time *(as appropriate)*. We work at... *(site)*. We are very proud of.... We are currently developing... .

   We are very keen for our children to learn all about their local environment and community. We should like to develop as many links as possible with the people who work or live in our area. The children would also like the local community to know about their setting and the work that they do there. We enclose one of our brochures that will give you a flavour of what we do at Rainbow Days.

   We should like to invite you, or one of your representatives, to visit us on... for *(tea/coffee/ a snack lunch)* to find out more about us and to see if we could establish some good links between us. If you are unable to visit us at this time, or would prefer some of our staff to visit you instead, would you please contact ... *(named staff member)* at ... *(telephone or contact)* to make mutually convenient arrangements.

   We hope to hear from you very soon.

➤ For the remaining time, give out the sheets of headed notepaper to the staff and ask them to write the letters inviting the agreed contacts to visit your setting.

➤ Remember to add your setting's brochure to the addressed envelopes.

Further action

➤ Send out the invitations and hold the meetings. Explore possible visits for the children, sponsorship for resources or projects, and the likelihood of visitors coming to talk about their company's work or personal interests.

A check-list for your setting concerning the issues raised in **Chapter 4** Working with parents and the community

➤ How many parents do you have working in your setting?

➤ What is the pattern of their help – regularly/occasionally/for trips/when asked?

➤ If you have difficulty attracting and maintaining parents' regular help, why is this? How might you overcome the problem?

➤ How do you manage too many parents anxious to help?

➤ Do you have a 'register' of parents and what they might be prepared to do to help?

➤ What strategies do you use to involve new parents?

➤ How do you involve working parents?

➤ Do you have any 'home-learning' packs or materials? How are these organised?

➤ Are all six Areas of Learning covered, including physical and creative activities?

➤ How are these materials updated and adapted for individual children?

➤ Can the children take books and other materials home if they are interested?

➤ How good are your communications with parents?

➤ Is this just with some or with all parents?

➤ How do you communicate with hard-to-contact parents?

➤ What do the parents think of the quality of your communications system? How do you know?

➤ What is the quality of your written communications, including brochures and booklets? Are they bright, attractive and user-friendly?

➤ What impression would new parents gain from these?

➤ Are there any gaps in communication?

➤ What do other settings do to improve parental communications? What do your 'feeder' colleagues do?

➤ Can you adopt any useful practices?

➤ How many visitors do you have to your setting? What do they do?

➤ How are these visitors planned into the programme?

➤ How do you use visitors to extend the children's learning?

➤ Are they representative of your locality and the pluralist society at large?

➤ How are visitors prepared, supported and valued in your setting?

➤ Which Areas of Learning would benefit from visitors, if possible?

➤ How do you use your wider community in your locality?

➤ What visits do you make with your children? What other visits might be possible?

➤ How does the local community know what you do in your setting?

➤ How do you 'market' yourselves?

➤ Do you exhibit the children's work in shops and libraries?

➤ Do you display brochures and information in public places, such as libraries?

➤ What links do you have with 'feeder' schools and settings? How might these be extended?

➤ Have you consulted parents for any community ideas and links that they may be able to offer?

➤ What schemes exist for artists in residence, musical groups, theatre groups and so on through your local education authority?

➤ Have you discussed ideas with your teacher-mentor and other colleagues in the area?

Chapter 5 Self-review and evaluation

Self-review and evaluation are key components of development in any early years setting. All the staff need to become confident in conducting regular reviews of the quality of their work and the overall provision of your setting

The staff need to carry out systematic reviews of aspects of their work and the impact that it has on learning. It is vital to create a healthy, safe 'no blame' approach so that the staff see the review process as a creative tool that enables them to do their jobs even more effectively.

Positive self-review

The first activity on page 66 introduces the concept of self-review with a very positive stance. It focuses on identifying what your setting does well, but emphasises the need to have definite evidence for your judgements. This session helps staff to look at the impact of your setting's approach and organisation on learning. It also offers advice on preparing evidence for OFSTED inspectors!

The positive theme is continued in the activity on page 68 which, helps the staff to highlight their own and others' best practice. The session is designed so that all the staff are active in the evaluation process, considering a range of the everyday practice within your setting. It provides a safe vehicle for the staff to consider how other settings tackle different aspects of work and will help you to decide how to adapt your own practice.

Areas requiring attention

In the activity on page 70, the focus is firmly on how to identify and prioritise areas where further attention is needed. This session takes a close look at the progress of individual children and the evidence that can be found in their work for making this judgement. Once more, this is a useful preparation for inspection and can provide clear evidence of your evaluation processes.

The activity on page 72 concerns the sensitive, but essential, area of reviewing the quality of teaching and learning. All the staff are usually involved in some form of teaching and learning with young children and this session is designed for whole-staff participation. It enables the staff to discuss in detail how they plan and carry out teaching activities, and helps them to consider how best to meet the needs of different children. The activity can be used regularly as part of self-review. Again, this session will result in useful evidence for OFSTED inspectors.

Best practice

Emphasis is given to personal review and recognition of staff's own best practice in the activity on page 74. The training unit covers two sessions, in order to give the staff time to reflect on their own work and share successful work with their colleagues, thus giving everyone a bank of new ideas to incorporate into their future work.

Finally, the activity on page 76 provides a clear focus and framework for making the most of staff visits to other settings.

Developing our self-review

Look at ways to improve the quality of your setting's provision

☗☗ Number of staff

All. (It would also be beneficial to invite any linked members of the governing body, school Senior Management Team or other management representatives.)

⏱ Timing

Approximately 1 hour 30 minutes.

What you need

A copy of the photocopiable sheet on page 140 for each member of staff; enlarged copy of photocopiable sheet; pens; flipchart; felt-tipped pens.

What you do

➤ Explain that the aim of this session is to review the quality of your setting's provision and to identify the general strengths and weaknesses of key aspects of your work.

➤ Make a strong statement that schools and settings are expected to undertake a regular review of where they are in their development and that this should feed into future

Preparation

➤ Prepare the flipchart or large sheets of paper with the following titles, statements and questions:

Sheet 1

Self-review and evaluation

◆ The setting that knows itself well, strengths and weaknesses alike, is well on the way to generating continuous improvement.

◆ Regular self-review is a feature of professionally healthy and dynamic early years settings.

◆ Settings that can identify accurate strengths and weaknesses are well placed to take action to solve any problems.

Sheet 2 (leaving space for comments)

◆ What do we do really well?

◆ What are the strengths of our setting?

◆ How do we know?

◆ What evidence could we show others to prove it?

plans for improvement. In schools, this should feed into the overall School Improvement or Development Plan. In other settings, it is considered to be so important that self-appraisal forms a part of OFSTED nursery inspections, and it remains a key feature of good-quality provision.

➤ Reveal the first sheet of paper and affirm this by stressing the three key statements. Allow a few minutes for staff to make any comments but ensure that they all accept the positive nature of self-review.

➤ Next, reveal the second sheet of paper and ask the staff to spend two or three minutes in pairs discussing the questions. As a group, discuss one area that you feel is a real strength of your setting. After a few minutes, jot down the two most definite and agreed suggestions in the space below the question.

➤ Now highlight the question 'How do we know?'. Take approximately ten to 15 minutes to work through this section. Refer to each of the original written suggestions at a time. Ask how the staff know that these are real strengths. Encourage the staff to focus on how the children learn and achieve. For example, if the staff say that 'Creative development' is a strength, ask them how they can tell from what the children are learning. Add their final conclusions to the space below the question.

➤ Finally, turn to the question 'What evidence could we show others to prove it?' Spend approximately ten minutes on this section. Explain that the staff have given their reasons for considering certain areas as strengths, now consider how a visitor to the setting would view things. If governors or other managers are present, their contributions would be valuable here. They might also like to ask questions about what they might see during a visit.

➤ Also ask the staff to suggest what evidence there might be over time that would confirm their own judgement about strengths. For example, are there photographs of activities, examples of the children's work, records of children's attainment and so on?

➤ Now give a copy of the photocopiable sheet to each member of staff. Ask them to work on their own for ten minutes, completing the grid. Allow them to move around the setting if they need to look for ideas. Let visitors use the time to explore your setting. If appropriate, they can have a sheet and complete part of the grid

personally.

➤ Bring the whole group together and ask the staff to spend ten minutes sharing their ideas in pairs or small groups, letting any visitors join in. Ask them to select their agreed major strengths and weaknesses.

➤ Turn to your enlarged copy of the photocopiable sheet. For the remaining time, let each pair feed back to the whole group and allow discussion and questions from other colleagues. When an agreement is reached, complete the grids on your large copy.

➤ If further time is needed, stop the activity at a suitable juncture and agree a date for a follow-up session to complete the task.

➤ Thank the staff for their thorough contributions. Explain that these will be converted into fair copies for all the staff and will also go into your overall 'Self-review file'.

Further action
➤ Make fair copies of your completed grid. Add the date and names of the staff and visitors involved in the review. You should now have a valuable starting-point for your self-review and evaluation, and have clearly identified areas of which you are proud, as well as areas where more attention is needed.

➤ Start, or add to, a 'Self-review file' and insert a copy as good evidence for inspectors! Ensure that all the staff receive a copy for their own records. Also provide copies for governors and other managers so that they can add these to the overall setting's files or their own management records.

➤ Use this information to move on to the next vital steps – action for sustaining good provision and improving perceived weaker areas. You should have reviewed your provision but now you need to plan a schedule to follow up your evaluations. It will be useful to undertake the other activities in this chapter.

Identifying best practice

Focus on establishing and sharing ideas as a whole group

👪 Number of staff

All.

🕐 Timing

1 hour.

What you need

Two copies of the photocopiable sheet on page 141 for each member of staff; pens; postcards; flipchart; felt-tipped pens; the *Curriculum Guidance for the Foundation Stage* (QCA) (available from QCA Publications, tel: 01787 884444); other available early years reference materials.

What you do

➤ Explain that the aims of this session are to consider how best practice can be identified and to consider ways to share and adopt the best ideas universally.

➤ Show the group the first sheet of paper on the flipchart and spend five minutes reading through the headings. Share the notion that if two people each have a penny and they swap them, they still have a penny each – but if they each have a good idea and they swap them, each one now has two good ideas!

Preparation

➤ Prepare the flipchart as follows:

Sheet 1

Identifying best practice

♦ All effective settings evaluate the quality of their work regularly.

♦ Successful settings accept that we can all improve.

♦ If we can identify what works really well, we can all share ideas and consistently replicate best practice.

Sheet 2

Identifying our best practice

Within all settings there are examples of really effective practice. Sometimes we are too busy to see it or share it!

♦ How do we discover it?

♦ How do we know that it is effective?

♦ How can we share it and all adopt it?

Sheet 3

Identifying other's best practice

♦ How can we find out how others work really well?

♦ How do we compare with others?

♦ How can we adopt the best ideas?

➤ Prepare the postcards with the following titles, selecting or adding what is most pertinent to your setting:

♦ greeting children
♦ children and parents arriving
♦ circle time
♦ registration
♦ snack time
♦ story time
♦ role-play
♦ home group/key worker group time
♦ deployment of staff-directed activities
♦ free-choice activities
♦ outdoor play
♦ supporting new children
♦ involving parents in work
♦ lunchtime organisation
♦ changing activities
♦ maintaining good control
♦ parents collecting children
♦ children's care and welfare
♦ changing for PE/outdoors
♦ tidying up.

➤ Make a strong statement that however good a setting is, it is always possible to improve and refresh practices.

➤ Turn to the second sheet on the flipchart and highlight the first statement. Now spend five to ten minutes asking the group to address the questions, stressing that some practice will be working really well, but other areas may benefit from adjustment to make them even more effective. Note that sometimes it is small 'tweakings' that turn ordinary practice into best practice.

➤ Ask the staff to concentrate on stating their reasons for why they think that their practice is effective. Talk about evidence for effective practice in terms of the children's learning and their rate of progress. Add staff comments to the flipchart.

➤ Now reveal the third sheet of paper on the flipchart. Spend five to ten minutes reading through the questions together. Think of ways for the staff to discover how other settings work and make a list of these. Highlight how your setting can use the teacher-mentor, any available local education authority support, or links with other schools and settings that already exist.

➤ Hold up the *Curriculum Guidance for the Foundation Stage* (QCA) and remind the staff that there are excellent examples of how others work scattered throughout the guidance.

➤ Allow the staff the opportunity to discuss comparative practice they may have seen on visits or from previous experience. Ask them to refer to the impact of different methods and organisation on children's learning.

➤ Give a copy of the photocopiable sheet to each person and ask the staff to work in small groups. Read through the headings together and explain that each group will cover different areas. Then give each person at least two postcards. Invite the staff to take turns to act as scribe or leader.

➤ Encourage each leader to introduce one card and lead discussions on identifying best practice for this item. Ask everyone to share their current practice in detail, for example, how each one organises changing for PE.

➤ Ask them to consider effective practice that they have seen, read about or heard about – or ideas that they would like to try out.

➤ Invite all the staff to agree their ideas and then help the scribe to fill in each photocopiable sheet. Spend up to 30 minutes on this task, completing all the cards and sheets.

➤ Spend the remaining time together. Encourage the scribes to read their cards and feed back their group's ideas. Make a note of the best practice ideas plus any requested visits, links or research.

➤ Conclude by thanking each person for their contributions and celebrate the areas of good practice!

Further action

➤ Add the final list of identified best practice to your 'Self-review file' and plan a list of activities for a follow-up session. For example, talk to your teacher-mentor or other colleagues and arrange a programme of visits to see other settings, focusing in on how well your best practice, in a precise area, compares with theirs. Offer reciprocal visits to support their professional development.

➤ Busy practitioners often do not have enough time to research alternative good practice. Develop a staff reference library of books, articles and specialist magazines. Hold occasional 'reading time' staff meetings where everyone can spend some time reading and then feed back two or three interesting ideas that they have collected to the whole group.

Identifying areas for development

Establish how children are making progress in the six Areas of Learning

✿ Number of staff
All.

🕐 Timing
I hour.

What you need
A copy of the photocopiable sheet on page 142 for each member of staff; pens; flipchart; felt-tipped pens; examples of the same children's work in an Area of Learning, Baseline or entry assessments; Post-it notes or similar; large space.

What you do
➤ Explain to the staff that the aim of this training session is to check how well your setting is doing at helping the children to make progress in the different Areas of Learning. The particular focus will be on looking at evidence of the children's learning from work sources.

Preparation
➤ If possible, undertake the activities 'Developing our self-review' on page 66 and 'Identifying best practice' on page 68 before carrying out this training unit, so that positive foundations for self-review have been already established.
➤ Identify six children from each year group or home base group in three general categories – of average ability, below average level and above average (two children in each band). Arrange for the widest possible selection of work and information from a specified Area of Learning to be brought to the training session. This Area of Learning can be one that you have already identified as needing attention, or may have been identified by OFSTED inspectors.
➤ If you are starting from scratch, begin with Communication, language and literacy (emergent writing, name writing, teacher as scribe, examples of pencil control, records of phonic knowledge and so on).
➤ Ask the staff to annotate this work sample using Post-it notes.
➤ Encourage them to state for each child and work example:
♦ the broad ability group (as above, marked 'A/BA/AA') and age

♦ the context of the work activity
♦ how it was produced (aided, unaided, copied, scribed and so on)
♦ any key points of the child's approach to it (directed, self-chosen, confident, keen, poor pencil control and so on).
➤ Prepare the flipchart with the following:

Sheet 1
Identifying areas for development
♦ Effective setting regularly appraise their own work critically and honestly.
♦ Effective settings also appraise the work of other providers and consider new approaches.
♦ It is a sign of professional strength for settings to recognise areas of their work that need more attention, and then to take steps to improve the children's learning.

Sheet 2
Key questions for self-review
♦ Are all the children in our setting, regardless of ability, learning as much as they are capable of learning?
♦ What can we do to find out?
♦ What do we do about it when we know the answer?

Staff training activities

early years
training &
management

➤ Refer to the first sheet of paper on the flipchart and spend a few minutes reading through the headings. Stress that the activities are strictly 'no blame' tasks, looking for a way forward for the whole setting, building on your current overall success.

➤ Now look at the second sheet on the chart. Explain that these questions are close to those in the *Handbook for Inspecting Primary and Nursery Schools* (OFSTED) and form a useful basis for self-review. Read through the headings together for approximately five minutes and discuss ways in which the staff could 'find out' the answers. List these on the chart. Point out that there are many sources of evidence.

➤ Explain that you are going to review work samples together to see what these tell you about the progress that the children of different abilities make over time.

➤ Give a copy of the photocopiable sheet to each person and read through the different sections together, highlighting the kind of information that they should put in each one. Decide the key things that you will look for. For example, in Communication, language and literacy you may want to look at specific elements of developing writing, such as correct letter formation, positioning and control; phonic awareness in spelling; and a range of different types of writing.

➤ Invite the staff to spread their work sample out on a large surface, with the children of the same age kept together, but sorted into ability samples.

➤ Ask the staff to work in pairs to discuss the sample material, starting with the youngest children first. Let them take approximately 30 minutes overall for this task. Encourage the

staff to begin by looking at any entry assessment information available and note attainment when they joined your setting.

➤ Next, invite the staff to focus on the average ability work. Ask them to go through this, looking for signs of progress. Complete the sections on the photocopiable sheet. Then repeat the task with the below average children and finally the above average sample. Ask the staff to look for work that is matched to ability and helps them to progress appropriately.

➤ Repeat the task for the other age groups. Let the staff complete the 'More evidence we need' section and then join together again.

➤ For the remaining time, ask each pair to feed back their main conclusions, suggesting which areas work well, but where more attention is needed to improve some aspects of learning. Remind the group that you are looking for ways that all the staff can help children make better progress overall.

➤ On the flipchart, note any areas that need more attention and then gather in the staffs' suggestions of how to do this. (Refer back to the third question on the second sheet on the flipchart.) Agree the actions that everyone will take, as well as dates to implement the changes.

Further action

➤ Circulate agreed actions to all the staff and ask them to build these into their planning. Consult your teacher-mentor or local colleagues and try to arrange an 'idea-gathering visit' to settings where they have a strength in your focus area.

➤ Revisit the task in a month or two and look for evidence of improvement. Repeat this exercise for the other Areas of Learning, over time.

Reviewing teaching and learning

Concentrate on the quality of teaching within your setting

Number of staff

All.

Timing

I hour 30 minutes – can be split into two sessions.

What you need

A copy of the photocopiable sheet on page 143 for each member of staff; pens; flipchart; felt-tipped pens; copies of next week's planning; paper; Blu-Tack.

What you do

➤ Take a few minutes to explain that all the staff in your setting contribute towards the quality of teaching. This needs to be productive for learning because each person makes a difference to the quality of experience that young children receive. Remind the staff that OFSTED inspections observe *all* staff in settings – teachers, nursery nurses, classroom assistants, specialist support staff and even volunteer helpers.

➤ Spend approximately 15 minutes reading through the 'Features of

Preparation

➤ Prepare the flipchart with the following, using one colour for the main text and another for the bracketed sections:
Features of effective teaching

1 The teacher plans effectively and there are clear learning objectives
(the children know what they are learning about, there is a good structure to the activity, materials are ready and appropriate, children with SEN are catered for appropriately, staff plan together well).

2 The teacher shows a good understanding of the needs of the Foundation Stage children
(tasks are appropriate for young children and capture their interest, timings and pace are suitable, children are active in their learning, the subject content is well understood by the teacher, support staff are used well).

3 The teaching methods enable all the children to learn effectively
(the children's ideas and experiences are built

on, a variety of activities and questioning is used, instructions and explanations are clear for the age group, all children are involved, high standards are encouraged, tasks are differentiated appropriately).

4 The children are well managed and good behaviour is insisted upon
(the children are praised and encouraged, poor behaviour is consistently addressed, all children are treated with equality of opportunity to learn, there is good organisation that the children understand and follow).

5 The children's progress is assessed and work is adapted to extend learning
(approaches and questions are altered in the light of assessment, mistakes are used constructively and recognised as stages of learning).

➤ When completed, cover the bracketed sections with easily removed paper screens using Blu-Tack.

effective teaching' as listed on the flipchart, keeping the bracketed sections covered. Ask the staff to suggest examples from their current work to illustrate each one.

➤ After each point, reveal the bracketed section and see how closely their ideas matched. If the staff have thought of additional points, congratulate them and add these to the list!

➤ Next, give a copy of the photocopiable sheet to each person. Spend approximately ten minutes discussing the various headings. Particularly concentrate on: 'What do I want the children to learn, experience and improve?' and highlight the difference between an activity and the learning objective behind it. For example, a sand-tray activity may be planned because it is a usual task for the Foundation Stage. However, the staff must consider how this will extend children's learning. Ask: 'What do I want the children to experience, discover and learn? What skills can be improved by this activity?'.

➤ Consider how the integrated nature of young children's learning will probably involve language development, and as the children often work together, Personal, social and emotional development may be implicit. Sand play, for example, could also involve Knowledge and understanding of the world through the exploration of different materials, Creative development through the stimulation and use of imagination, Mathematical development (if the appropriate containers are used) and Physical development through the extension of fine motor skills when using apparatus. A clear learning objective for the activity will help the staff to decide what specific equipment to use and how the task should be organised.

➤ Ask the staff to work in pairs, taking turns to take the lead. Allow 25 minutes for this task. Let each person choose a teaching session for the following day/week that they intend to deliver – whole class, group session or a particular activity.

➤ Let them talk through how they will plan and organise it, identifying the learning objectives and the required resources. In pairs, discuss the activity, share ideas and refine the session, completing the photocopiable grid together (up to the 'Evaluation and review' section).

➤ Join together for ten minutes to discuss progress and deal with any points that may have arisen.

➤ Explain that the staff should carry out the activity as planned and then spend a few minutes completing the evaluation sections of the sheet ready to bring back to the next staff training session. Stress that everyone needs to be honest as this is a learning experience for all – and the aim is to focus on making your teaching even more effective!

Further action

➤ Plan a follow-up session of approximately one hour. Distribute copies of everyone's completed photocopiable sheet. Let all the staff take turns to talk the group through their planned activity, especially highlighting how they would develop it further when they teach the session again. Encourage everyone to contribute ideas and suggestions.

➤ Give out fresh copies of the photocopiable sheet and ask the staff to repeat the process, selecting a different teaching session in the following week. Hold follow-up sessions to share successes and highlight areas for further development. Build in similar sessions, once or twice a term, to keep up a regular review.

➤ Keep a file of staff sheets, with dates of review sessions. This is good evidence of staff training for OFSTED appraisal or performance management!

Sharing best practice together

Find ways to share best practice effectively

✿ Number of staff
All.

🕐 Timing
Two 1-hour sessions.

What you need
A copy of the photocopiable sheet on page 144 for each member of staff; pens; flipchart; different-coloured felt-tipped pens; planning and past evidence of work (photographs, work samples and so on).

Preparation
➤ If possible, undertake the activity 'Identifying best practice' on page 68 before carrying out this training unit.
➤ Write out the following on the flipchart:
Sharing best practice together
♦ Early years settings have a rich source of best practice within their own environment.
♦ Busy practitioners do not often make time to share in detail what works well.
♦ We have to go outside our own setting to see best practice.
♦ Visits can give us fresh ideas.
♦ What works elsewhere will not work here.
♦ We all need time and opportunities to consider different approaches.
♦ Change can be exciting.
♦ What we do now works well enough.
♦ We have not got time to consider changing our provision.
♦ Children are just the same as they have always been.
♦ We need time to reflect on what we do and see if we can make it better.
♦ We all have special talents and expertise.
➤ Write out two copies of the photocopiable sheet on to separate sheets of paper on the flipchart. Leave the first one as headings only. Complete the second one (by doing the reflection activity yourself), using a different-coloured pen for the text. This will be used later as a model.

What you do
➤ Explain that the object of this training unit is to examine ways of sharing best practice productively and to set up a system that works in your setting and that the training unit is in two sessions – the first to prepare the ground and the second to start the process.

Session 1
➤ Turn to the statements on the flipchart and spend approximately ten minutes reading through each statement with the group. Encourage the staff to share their views, then decide whether they consider the comments to be true or false. Mark the chart in one colour for 'true' and an alternative colour for 'false'.
➤ Take a very positive lead as you go through the exercise. Listen to any negative comments but introduce a balance. For example, if the staff think that there is too little time to consider changes or reflect on provision, ask whether you can afford not to find the time for this essential activity. Point out that some things will have to be addressed as management issues to make sure that time is programmed.
➤ When discussing whether children have changed, highlight how society, parenting skills, legal requirements such as the SEN *Code of Practice* and the children's experiences have changed. (Focus on any issues in your own particular community such as unemployment, lone parents, working parents, lack of safe play areas and so on.)

➤ Make a strong statement about how it is important that all settings need to build on the best they can do – celebrating and extending the good practice, as well as being open to new ideas.

➤ Now introduce the main activity. Reveal the enlarged photocopiable sheet headings on the flipchart and read through these together. Emphasise the importance of the 'Outcomes to learning' section.

➤ Show the group the photocopiable grid that you completed earlier. Spend a few minutes talking to the staff through your model. Refer to any planning that you used and demonstrate any work, photographs or similar that you may have.

➤ Explain that each colleague should think of a recently completed, successful teaching or support activity. (Whole class, group or individual and linked to their particular roles.)

➤ Use the remaining time to reflect on why this was successful. Now give each member of staff a copy of the photocopiable sheet and ask them to fill it in to form the basis of a script for a presentation in Session 2. Ask them to work individually, referring to past planning.

➤ Circulate and give individual support, suggesting ideas of what you know they have done well – early years practitioners are often very modest! Encourage reflection on why their work resulted in good learning.

➤ Let the staff complete the sheets and gather work ready to present their ideas for the next session.

Session 2

➤ Briefly remind colleagues of the aim of the session. Draw lots for the running order of presentations – or

start with volunteers. Aim for approximately five to ten minutes for each presentation, with a few extra minutes for questions.

➤ Let each member of staff present their reflection on their chosen best practice activity, talking the group through each section.

➤ Encourage the staff to ask questions. If necessary, ask your own questions and support the staff member. For example, say 'I saw the group at work and was impressed by the way you...' or 'Can you tell us how you encouraged Marie to...?'.

➤ Thank each member of staff for their presentation. Compile a booklet containing all the completed sheets. Title it 'Sharing our best practice' and circulate copies to all members of staff.

Further action

➤ At each staff meeting, spend ten minutes focusing on best practice on an agreed topic. Write up all successful ideas and let the staff add these to a personal 'Best practice bank' file for future reference.

➤ Share your best practice booklet and 'Bank' with colleagues, teacher-mentors and so on, and ask for theirs in return.

Visiting other settings

Consider the advantages of visiting other early years settings

Number of staff
All.

Timing
Approximately I hour for the first session, plus follow-up feedback sessions.

What you need
A copy of the photocopiable sheet on page 145 for each member of staff; pens; flipchart; different-coloured felt-tipped pens.

Preparation
➤ If possible, undertake the activities 'Identifying best practice' on page 68 and 'Ideas for development' on page 70 before carrying out this training unit.
➤ On the flipchart, prepare the following:

Sheet 1
Making the most of visits to other settings
♦ Visits to other settings enable practitioners to look at different ways of doing things.
♦ Visits elsewhere help you to reflect on your own work.
♦ Visits can give you opportunities to stand back and watch other skilled staff working in different circumstances.

Sheet 2
Making visits to other settings
♦ Advantages.
♦ Disadvantages.

Sheet 3
What we need to focus on to help our development
(If this has already been discussed and agreed from earlier activities in this chapter, have these areas already written here. If not, leave this section blank with space to add specific items.)
♦ How we can find this out.
♦ Things to look for.

What you do
➤ Explain that the aim of this session is to identify the most useful things to focus on for any visits that will be made to other settings. Make strong statements to underline the value of well-handled visits. Stress that it is vital to get the maximum benefits from the precious (and expensive in real terms) time spent on visits during setting operation sessions. Each visit, therefore, needs careful planning to ensure that all the staff benefit from the information and insights gained.
➤ Reveal the first sheet of paper on the flipchart. Spend a few minutes going through the headings together and reaffirming the opportunities presented for visiting staff.
➤ Now turn to the second sheet of paper and ask the staff to spend ten minutes or so discussing the advantages and disadvantages of making visits and filling in the flipchart. If necessary, ask a few pertinent questions to encourage discussion. For example, ask 'Is it an advantage or disadvantage to visit a setting in a very different area?' or 'Is it an advantage or disadvantage not to know the children?'.
➤ Complete the table and then go back through the disadvantages list. Ask the staff to think how the disadvantages could be addressed positively. In a different-coloured pen, jot down practical ideas to resolve any disadvantages. For example, if a disadvantage is not knowing much about the setting's context or organisation, could you request information or a brochure to

study before the visit is made? Also look at the advantages and try to identify any pre-visit preparations or reading that would be useful. Take approximately ten minutes for this.

➤ Look at the third sheet of paper on the flipchart. Spend approximately 15 minutes discussing and agreeing the areas that your setting needs to develop, or compare practice in.

➤ Concentrate on the 'How can we find this out?' section. Spend five minutes asking the staff to suggest all the different things that they could look for which would give useful information in the areas that you want to improve.

➤ Work through one idea, for example, if you are concerned about improving Creative development, make a list of things that would help you to reach an understanding of what the setting does (such as groups, planning for the week and longer term, displays, the children's work and resources). Or, if improving the organisation of free-choice activities was the intended focus, consider what exactly would need to be observed and how the staff could best go about it.

➤ Add brightly coloured asterisks to note where you may need to contact the setting you are planning to visit in advance to see whether you can make your intended observations.

➤ Now give a copy of the photocopiable sheet to each member of staff. Ask them to work in pairs and allocate one of the focus areas for visits to each group. Explain that they will use the remaining time to complete a 'Visit preparation' sheet for their specific developmental area and that fair copies of these will be given to the staff to use when they make the arranged visits.

Follow-up sessions

➤ It is essential to plan some time after each visit for the staff to feed back, using the 'Visit preparation' sheet as an agenda to report from. The staff take their sheet with them, adding comments and information from their visit in a different coloured pen.

➤ Allow at least 30 minutes for staff to present their reports and for questions from colleagues.

➤ On the flipchart, make a note of any implications for your setting, required further consideration and research as well as agreed and dated actions.

Further action

➤ Before finalising the details for any visits, sensitively discuss the extra information that you require, such as the setting's brochure, planning, the day's timetable of activities and so on. Arrange for this information to be available.

➤ Prepare a 'Visiting colleague's pack' for your own setting and offer this to the setting that you plan to visit. In this, outline the context of your setting, general organisation, patterns of the day, planning format examples and other useful information – including domestic issues such as parking! Be brave enough to also state those areas that you feel you do very well! Give a copy to your teacher-mentor.

A check-list for your setting concerning the issues raised in **Chapter 5** Self-review and evaluation

➤ Do we have a regular and systematic way of reviewing the quality of our provision?

➤ Are review dates planned in as part of our termly and annual staff meetings?

➤ How do we decide which aspects of our work to focus on for review?

➤ Who is involved in the review?

➤ What happens to the outcomes of our reviews?

➤ Who is this information shared with?

➤ How do we keep records of this review, staff participation and outcomes?

➤ Have we started a 'Self-review file' and do we make this available for inspectors and other relevant colleagues such as governors and managers?

➤ Do we revisit the review and ascertain what difference any of our agreed actions have made?

➤ Is our review and evaluation firmly rooted in the effects of our work on children's learning?

➤ How do we regularly review individual children's progress?

➤ Do we share samples of work together and discuss what the children need to do next?

➤ Do we make time to discuss and share our own best practice together?

➤ What system do we have for the staff to review their own work?

➤ How is this shared with managers?

➤ How do we celebrate our successes and best practices?

➤ Do we plan and spend time discussing best practice as demonstrated in other settings, or set out in the *Curriculum Guidance for the Foundation Stage* (QCA) or other similar reference materials?

➤ Are we developing a staff library of books and suitable reference materials that will extend our own knowledge of good practice?

➤ Can we plan in some staff 'reading time' sessions to help the process along?

➤ How do we decide which areas of our work need further development?

➤ How do we prioritise these and ensure that we attend to the ones that will make the greatest improvement to the children's learning first?

➤ How do we keep ourselves on track to attend to priorities and not get side-tracked by other events?

➤ How do we organise visits to other settings?

➤ Do we ask our teacher-mentor about best practice and where to find it?

➤ Do we consult other agencies such as health services, social services, the local education authority and so on, about where to find best practice in specific areas?

➤ How many visits have been made to other settings?

➤ What have been the benefits for us?

➤ Have we adopted – or adapted – any ideas that we have seen working elsewhere?

➤ How do we prepare before a visit?

➤ How do we know what to look for when we are at other settings?

➤ How do those staff who have made visits share their observations with their colleagues on their return?

➤ Are visits restricted to only certain categories of staff or does everyone have a chance to make a visit over time?

Chapter 6 Inspection issues

Although the inspection process has been established for some time, it is an area that causes some anxiety for all early years settings! This chapter will help you to prepare for your inspection with confidence.
In school-based settings, the process spans over a few days with several inspectors contributing to the final report. In other settings, the process is limited to one inspector for a more limited, but intense, visit, with feedback at the end of the day.

Preparing for inspection
All the ideas in this book are a valuable resource as an ongoing preparation for OFSTED inspections. However this chapter is devoted specifically to helping settings prepare for their OFSTED inspection in a positive manner, with many practical strategies for collecting powerful evidence to present to inspectors. Inspectors are usually pleased to receive such evidence as they are aware that they only witness a small part of your setting's work, yet need to comment on much broader areas.

Different settings
There are differences between the inspection processes for schools and other settings. The first activity on page 80 is aimed at enabling primary and nursery schools to make appropriate preparations for re-inspection, as well as providing valuable evidence for inspectors.

The activity on page 82 is designed for private, voluntary and

independent settings who undergo OFSTED inspections as part of the requirements for receiving grant aid. This activity should help these settings to prepare for re-inspections and produce good evidence of a careful review of progress for your registered nursery inspector.

Sharing success
It is important for settings to celebrate and share their successes with inspectors. The activity on page 84 is appropriate for all settings and focuses on building staff confidence in recognising and recording those things that your setting does well. It also gives useful suggestions for how this information can be shared with inspectors, and used to inform other key people who may be involved in the inspection process – managers, other colleagues and parents. Similarly, a positive approach to dealing with your weaker areas is covered in the activity on page 86 and this should prove to inspectors that your setting evaluates its work realistically.

Issues concerning the inspection visit itself are dealt with in the activity on page 88. This session gives a very practical approach, involving all the staff in their final preparations. It also focuses on helping everyone to feel as positive as possible, despite nervousness!

Finally, the activity on page 90 provides a training session to help settings cover necessary post-inspection requirements as a whole staff – preparing workable action plans and laying out a clear pathway for future developments.

Preparing for re-inspection

(Primary and nursery schools)

👪 Number of staff
All (linked governors and senior managers could be involved).

🕐 Timing
I hour I5 minutes.

What you need
A copy of the photocopiable sheet on page 146 for each member of staff; pens; flipchart; felt-tipped pens; copy of your last inspection report; two different-coloured highlighter pens; the school or phase's post-OFSTED action plan; any early years or Foundation Stage action plans; Post-it notes or similar.

What you do
➤ Explain that the aim of this session is to check on progress since the last inspection, and to start preparations for the next one. By the end of the session, everyone should be familiar with the last inspection findings and have a clear idea of current progress. Stress that this is a useful checkpoint for development, even if the next inspection date is not yet known.
➤ Reveal the first sheet of paper on the flipchart and spend ten minutes reading through the positives. Be aware that you may have new staff since this inspection, or new staff

Preparation
➤ Read through the subject section of your inspection report on 'Areas of Learning for children in the Foundation Stage' (early reports may refer to 'under-fives') and highlight all the positive comments in one colour and all the negatives in the second colour.
➤ On the flipchart, prepare the following, summarising the highlighted comments under the appropriate headings.
Sheet 1
Previous inspection – what went well.
Sheet 2
Previous inspection – what needed attention.
(Briefly put the date and details on to the top section of the photocopiable sheet before you make copies for everyone.)
➤ Read through the first part of the inspection report looking at the whole-school issues and highlight the positive and

negative judgements that have a link with early years, as well as other areas of the school. For example, comments on teaching, curriculum, resources and management may also affect the Foundation Stage. If there is a judgement that children with special needs are well supported, or more able children are not challenged enough, the Foundation Stage needs to play its part in sustaining or improving standards.
Sheet 3
Previous inspection – whole school issues that we need to consider.
Positives.
Negatives.
➤ Look at the final key issues and list these, highlighting them with implications for the Foundation Stage and staff.
Sheet 4
Whole-school key issues for improvement.

Staff training activities

early years
training & management

that have never experienced an inspection – so allow time for questions and explanations.

➤ Move on to the second sheet of paper on the flipchart and take another ten minutes or so to read through the particular areas for attention for the Foundation Stage. Be sensitive to the concerns of new and long-standing staff, but point out that inspectors will prepare for their work by analysing the previous report, and then seek to follow up how the setting has tackled any identified weaknesses.

➤ Stress the whole-staff approach to improvement, avoid any 'blame culture' – even if there were difficulties at the time of the last inspection. Keep honest but positive!

➤ Present the third sheet on the flipchart and discuss any of the other aspects of the inspection that might affect the Foundation Stage.

➤ Turn to the fourth sheet of paper on the flipchart and refer to the key issues. Pay particular attention to any that have a direct bearing on the work of the Foundation Stage or staff within it. Discuss any implications. Take approximately ten minutes for this task.

➤ Now give a copy of the photocopiable sheet to each member of staff and spend five minutes reading through the headings. Explain that you have filled in the top section to match the second sheet on the flipchart for them.

➤ Ask the staff to work in pairs or small groups to discuss each issue and to decide how it has been dealt with, or what still remains to be done, completing the rest of the photocopiable sheet. (If possible, arrange to have mixed groups comprising new staff and staff who were present at the last inspection.)

➤ Encourage the staff to be honest, but to also think widely about what has been done. It is common for busy practitioners to forget what they have done! Allow 20 minutes for this activity. Circulate to give support for all groups.

➤ For the remaining time, turn the flipchart back to the second sheet. Ask the staff to feed back their findings and write notes of these against the issues. For example:

♦ Insufficient outdoor play – new vehicles bought but more needed.

♦ Daily outdoor sessions,

♦ Limited use of hall if wet.

➤ Refer to any school or phase action plan to address these issues, read out the different sections and decide how much progress has been made against agreed intentions. Ask a member of staff to tick or cross the chart items as appropriate.

➤ Make a fresh list of things to do, chase up, or bring to the attention of senior management, for example, resource or timetable issues, and agree how, by whom, and when these will be done. Give everyone a Post-it note and ask them to write their own *aide mémoire* of what they have to do and put it on a prominent noticeboard!

➤ Arrange a further session to check on how these actions have been carried out.

Further action

➤ Keep all the photocopiable sheets as a record of your review and good evidence for inspectors. Inform senior management of the overall outcome of your review and request help where necessary.

➤ Update the photocopiable sheets just before your inspection and prepare two aggregated fair copies to take to any interviews. Leave one with the inspector.

Preparing for re-inspection

(Private, voluntary and independent settings)

❧ Number of staff
All, including managers.

⏱ Timing
Approximately 1 hour 15 minutes.

What you need
A copy of the photocopiable sheet on page 147 for each member of staff; pens; a copy of your last inspection report each member of staff; a copy of your action plan for each member of staff; flipchart; two different-coloured highlighter pens; felt-tipped pens; Post-it notes or similar; copy of the *Handbook for Inspecting Nursery Education in the Private, Voluntary and Independent Sectors* (OFSTED).

Preparation
➤ Read through your own inspection report and highlight all the positive comments in one colour and all the negatives in another.
➤ On the flipchart, summarise the highlighted comments under the appropriate heading.
Sheet 1
Previous inspection – what went well.
Sheet 2
Previous inspection – what needed attention.
Sheet 3
What our setting needed to do next.
(what had to be addressed in our post-inspection action plan)
➤ Familiarise yourself with the *Handbook for Inspecting Nursery Education in the Private, Voluntary and Independent Sectors* (OFSTED), particularly 'Part 1 The Inspection Framework' and 'What Inspectors and Contractors Must Do' (page 7 onwards).

What you do
➤ Explain to the staff that the aim of this session is to review progress that has been made since the time of the previous inspection and to prepare for the next. (Although the exact date of the next inspection may not be known, the previous inspection report will have given some indication of the approximate period when the next inspection can be expected.) Stress the importance of maintaining a regular review of issues to help your own general development and keep your setting on track – regardless of worrying about impending inspections!
➤ Ascertain how many staff were present for the previous inspection, how many are new to the setting and how many may have had inspection experience elsewhere. Say that this session should help everyone to be clear about the process and the current position of progress in your setting.
➤ Explain that inspectors refer to the previous inspection report and the required issues for improvement as a starting-point for their preparations and subsequent inspection visit to the setting.
➤ Give a copy of your previous inspection report to each member of staff. Spend approximately 25 minutes reading through the report together, section by section. After reading one paragraph, show the colour bands of highlighter on your own copy and explain the relative balance of strengths and weaknesses.
➤ Spend approximately ten minutes inviting the staff to share their experiences of inspection and how inspectors operated during the inspection visit. Refer to the *Handbook for Inspecting Nursery*

Education in the Private, Voluntary and Independent Sectors (OFSTED) and say that inspectors look at a whole range of other evidence in observed sessions – planning, the children's work, records, discussions with the staff, analysis of information from the manager, plus other available data. Stress that all this evidence goes towards forming overall judgements.

➤ As you read each section, make brief notes on the first and second sheet of paper on the flipchart, of the respective strengths and weaknesses.

➤ At the end of the entire report discuss 'What does the setting need to do next?', and write down the key issues for action on the third sheet of paper on the flipchart. Now distribute copies of your action plan and refresh the staff's memories, or introduce your intended strategies outlining the decisions made to address the identified areas for improvement.

➤ Show the staff the *Handbook for Inspecting Nursery Education in the Private, Voluntary and Independent Sectors* (OFSTED) and refer to page 25 – the need for inspectors to 'analyse the setting's performance since the last inspection including an evaluation of the progress made in implementing the action plan'. Take approximately 15 minutes to read through your action plan together, reviewing in outline what has been achieved so far.

➤ Give a copy of the photocopiable sheet to each member of staff and ask them to work in pairs or small groups. (If possible, mix the staff that are new to the setting with longer-serving staff.) Ask the staff to work through the photocopiable sheet together, completing all the sections, referring to the different sheets, and

the action plan, but most importantly, using their own knowledge of their work within the setting. Take 20 minutes for this task.

➤ For the remaining time, gather the group back together and let each pair feed back their ideas. Refer once more to the second and third sheet of paper on the flipchart and decide how much progress has been made against each point. Put a tick where an issue has been completely addressed and a cross where progress is still not fully made.

➤ Make notes against each item, with explanations or important comment. For example, 'Increase the use of instruments in Creative development – more instruments purchased, staff training undertaken, instruments used regularly in groups'.

➤ Make a list of outstanding tasks that need to be tackled. Include specific things to do, decisions to be made by managers, resources that are needed, training implications and so on. Decide how and when these things will be done and by whom, and make a master list. Give out the Post-it notes and ask all the relevant staff to write themselves an *aide mémoire* of what they have to do to stick in their diaries.

➤ Arrange a further session to check that these actions are carried out and to address any constraints.

Further action

➤ Keep the photocopiable sheets as evidence of review for inspectors. Use the aggregated information to complete the paperwork that you need to send to the inspector before the visit, or keep it ready for the required time.

➤ Gather together evidence in the children's work, planning, staff training records and so on to support your views of progress to date.

Maximising strengths

Consider ways to provide positive evidence of your setting's provision

༤༤༤ Number of staff
All, also suitable for managers and linked governors.

⏱ Timing
45 minutes.

What you need
A copy of your previous inspection report; copy of your post-OFSTED action plan; sheet of A1 card; several sheets of A1 sugar paper; large adhesive labels (address type); pens; examples of the children's good-quality work in an Area of Learning that you consider you do well; samples of letters home to parents and carers; photographs of a wide range of your setting's activities; scissors; glue; flipchart; felt-tipped pens.

What you do
➤ Explain that the aim of this session is to prepare for inspection by sharing examples of work that you feel are the strengths of your provision. Stress that, depending on the time of your inspection, inspectors may only observe a fraction of what you cover over an annual cycle. It is important to give yourselves credit for what you believe you do well – but you will need to have actual evidence for this!
➤ Remind the staff that inspectors will be keen to report on all the Areas of Learning and aspects of your provision required by OFSTED.

Preparation
➤ It would be beneficial to have undertaken the activities 'Identifying best practice' on page 68 and 'Sharing best practice together' on page 74 before carrying out this training unit, as you will already have a good basis to build on. Have the completed 'Best practice' phoptocopiable sheets or compiled 'Best practice bank' available for staff reference.
➤ Fold the sheets of card and sugar paper in half and put together to make a large book. Add the title 'Our setting's success' to the front page.
➤ Prepare the flipchart as follows:

Sheet 1
For nursery and primary schools
OFSTED reporting requirements
Evaluations of
♦ the standards achieved and the extent to which children are on course to reach the expected outcomes (Early Learning Goals)
in all six Areas of Learning
Personal, social and emotional development
Communication, language and literacy
Mathematical development
Knowledge and understanding of the world
Physical development
Creative development.
♦ any differences in provision or attainment for children who are five or under in the nursery, reception or mixed-age classes – and why.
♦ the quality of teaching
♦ changes since the previous inspection
♦ any factors that have a bearing on what is achieved, such as quality of management, planned curriculum and use of time, resources and accommodation, parental partnerships, support for children with special needs and/or children with English as an additional language.

Sheet 2
For other settings
OFSTED reporting requirements
Evaluations of
♦ the effectiveness of the setting in terms of the quality it provides for funded three- and four-year-olds.
♦ how well the funded three- and four-year olds learn in each of the six Area of Learning:
Personal, social and emotional development
Communication, language and literacy
Mathematical development
Knowledge and understanding of the world
Creative development
Physical development
♦ how the setting has improved since the previous activity
♦ what the setting does well
♦ what it needs to do to improve
♦ how well the children are taught and what makes it successful in promoting the children's progress (including children with SEN or EAL).
♦ the effectiveness of partnerships with parents and carers
♦ recommendation for the timing of the next inspection.
♦ Plan the session well ahead and ask the staff to retain and bring along examples of the children's work in an area that they are proud of – including work that demonstrates successful support for children with special needs or high ability, plus supporting photographs and planning, examples of work with parents, visitors and visits.

If there is little or no evidence in any area, they may conclude the provision is unsatisfactory.

➤ Reveal the appropriate flipchart sheet for your setting and spend approximately 15 minutes reading through the headings. For each point, ask the staff to suggest evidence of strong provision in your setting that would be useful, and note this on the chart.

➤ For the remaining time, ask the staff to work in pairs (or small groups) and give each pair a folded sheet of sugar paper. Explain that they will start to compile pages for the 'Successes' book. Remind the staff of (or discuss and agree) those aspects of provision that you do well and allocate one of these to each pair.

➤ Ask the staff to sort work samples, photographs or other evidence and glue it to their sheets, using the adhesive labels to add titles, explanations, references to planning and dates.

➤ Make a note of any missing evidence and agree how this will be covered. Decide who will be responsible for obtaining it and adding it to the book. For example, entry assessment information analysis, a specimen of planning for a seasonal activity, a brief staff account of an event or visit, arranging to take photographs, collecting parents' views and so on. Set deadlines for action.

Further action

➤ If necessary, hold a follow-up session to complete the process. Check the contents and add any further notes of clarification. Complete the book and clip it firmly together or transfer the contents to a large A2 ring-binder file. Keep it ready to give to inspectors. Be prepared to add extra pages to it as time goes on.

➤ This book can also be useful to inform managers, parents, teacher-mentors and other visitors about your provision. Appropriate visual sections could be reproduced in brochures or the governors' 'Annual report to parents'!

Approaches to weaknesses

Focus on positive approaches to address any shortcomings in your setting

✸ Number of staff
All, also relevant for managers and linked governors.

⏱ Timing
Approximately 1 hour.

What you need
A copy of the photocopiable sheet on page 148 for each member of staff, mounted on to card; pens; flipchart; felt-tipped pens; scissors; Blu-Tack; your action plan from the activity 'Planning for the future' on page 20.

Preparation
➤ It is important to undertake the activity 'Planning for the future' on page 20 before carrying out this training unit. Your audits and findings from the other chapters could also beneficially feed into this session.
➤ Prepare the flipchart as follows:

Sheet 1
Positive approaches to weaknesses
◆ It is a very rare setting that has no areas that require extra attention.
◆ A setting that knows its weaknesses is in a good position to do something positive about them!
◆ It is a sign of strength to know what you need help with.
◆ We can show inspectors that we are positively tackling our weaker areas.

Sheet 2
List the main areas in your setting where development is needed (taken from the action plan).

What you do
➤ Explain to the staff that the aim of this session is to reaffirm the areas in your setting that need further development and also to highlight the positive actions for improvement that you have taken already.
➤ Look at the first sheet of paper on the flipchart and spend a few minutes reading through the statements emphasising the positive comments. Reassure the staff that inspectors will obviously find areas for further development – it is their job to help settings know what to focus on next. However, they will also recognise that a setting has the capacity to improve if they can see that staff are already working, or have firm plans in place, to tackle any weaker practice.
➤ If appropriate, remind the staff that they have covered much ground in previous training units from this book and should be well along the way to dealing with any weaker areas of provision in the setting. Make a strong statement that even if slow progress has been made so far, or action has only just been agreed, every definite step forward is positive. Any plans you have drawn up will indicate your firm intentions to inspectors. Staff, managers and governors need to be familiar with these priorities.
➤ Turn to the second sheet of paper on the flipchart and spend a little time reading through the list of areas that you and the staff have already decided need more work.
➤ Present your action plan from the activity 'Planning for the future' on page 20 and spend approximately ten minutes discussing each listed strategy, checking how much progress has been made to date.
➤ Next, take the first four areas for improvement from your action plan and write each one as a title on a separate sheet. Tear off each sheet and display it in an easily accessible position.

➤ Give a copy of the photocopiable sheet to each member of staff and ask them to work in pairs for this task.

➤ Invite the staff to cut out their eight flag and flagpole shapes. Encourage the pairs to discuss any ideas for helping the setting to make speedier progress on the first priority. Let each member of staff take a flag and write down one positive suggestion. Encourage them to think creatively and beyond the original action plan ideas.

➤ If improvement has been made, even in a small way, ask the staff to write this on a second flag, adding how they can tell this, for example, what evidence they have seen of progress. Ask them to attach their flags on to the appropriate priority sheet with Blu-Tack.

➤ Repeat the process for the other three priorities. Allow approximately 20 minutes for this activity.

➤ For the remaining time, present each completed priority sheet to the whole group and look at all the flags that feature progress.

➤ Celebrate the successes, however small. Then discuss all the ideas flags. Draw a ring around all those that are agreed as positive and manageable without overloading the staff. Try to indicate a time-scale when these could be implemented, such as 'immediately'; 'by the end of term'; or 'next year'. Stress that you cannot do everything at once and any additions need to be introduced in a staged and systematic approach which complements the original plan.

➤ Be sensitive towards any member of staff whose suggestions cannot be implemented because of unavoidable constraints such as insufficient time available, or resource or building limitations. Say, for example, 'It is unlikely that we can adopt that good

idea, however much we would like to! But can we think of a similar alternative that could work – or go part of the way towards it? Or could we keep that suggestion for a later review?'

➤ Conclude the session with thanks to the staff and explain that their contributions will be typed up and incorporated wherever possible into the revised action plan. Circulate the adjusted plan to all the staff and also to managers and governors as this will help everyone to have a clear picture of your setting's actions. This information will be essential in any feedback sessions with inspectors.

Further action
➤ Take the original action plan and write on it, in a contrasting pen so that it shows up clearly, the review date, the staff present and that new ideas have been added to an updated plan. Also add agreed progress comments on improvements to date, listing staff sources of evidence. Prepare the revised plan and have both ready for inspectors.

Dealing with the inspection visit

Consider how to plan and make provision for an inspector's visit

⚇ Number of staff
All, also useful for managers.

⊙ Timing
Approximately 1 hour.

What you need
A copy of the photocopiable sheet on page 149 for each member of staff; pens; the *Handbook for Primary and Nursery Schools* (OFSTED) or the *Handbook for Nursery Education in the Private, Voluntary and Independent Sectors* (OFSTED); large storage box; file for planning and other documents; flipchart; felt-tipped pens.

What you do
➤ Explain that the aim of this session is to help everyone prepare for the inspection visit and to plan what needs to be done together.
➤ Show the group sheet 1 on the flipchart. Make a strong statement, explaining that the inspection should be managed by yourselves being pro-active, rather than just having it happen to you!
➤ Start with the first heading on sheet 1 and bring out your 'Inspection Box'. Explain that all your policies and planning need to be

Preparation
➤ Carry out this training session at least three weeks before your inspection is due, to give the staff time to prepare. If you are a school, this is best done before the inspector makes the pre-inspection visit, because it is likely that inspectors will tour the school and they are already collecting information to put together a pre-inspection commentary to brief their teams. (This is also sent to schools just before the inspection.) Remember that you never get a second chance to make a first impression!
➤ Label the storage box 'Inspection box and the file 'Inspection documents'.
➤ Read through the relevant sections of the appropriate 'Handbook' and familiarise yourself with the procedures for before and during the inspection.
➤ Prepare the flipchart as follows:
Sheets 1 and 2 (leave a space under each heading for group comments)
What we need to do before the visit
♦ Have all our policies and documents ready.
♦ Collect our evidence of good practice together.

♦ Identify children who might 'read' to inspectors and collect samples of their work (school settings).
♦ Ensure that we have complete planning – check and share our planning so that everyone is clear about what to do.
♦ Make sure that all the activities are appropriate and have definite learning objectives.
♦ Ensure that all parents and helpers are properly briefed well in advance.
♦ Work out how we shall organise all groups and how support staff will be actively used.
♦ Identify and 'book' all necessary resources for activities.
♦ Agree 'rainy day' strategies.
♦ Check the area is as we want visitors to see it – displays, cloakrooms, storage.
♦ Declutter!
♦ Prepare the children for visitors.
Sheet 3
Arrange post-OFSTED treats!
Sheet 4
What we need to do during the visit
♦ Check that everything is ready in good time.

♦ Report any problems immediately.
♦ Concentrate on our teaching and the children's learning.
♦ Deal with any disruptions in the normal way such as behaviour

issues and welfare.
♦ Listen carefully to the inspectors' questions and comments.
♦ Support each other.
♦ Find some time to relax!

collected together in this container, ready to be given to inspectors.

➤ Take five minutes to gather all the staff's ideas of what policies and information should be included, and make a list If necessary, prompt them with admissions policy, induction programme, brochure, parents' information booklets, examples of record-keeping, Foundation Stage profile information and analysis, staff handbook, staff meeting minutes, training record and so on.

➤ Refer to the second heading on the first sheet of paper on the flipchart and ask for ideas of items that demonstrate evidence of your good practice – particularly if this will not be evident during the inspection visit. These should also go into the 'Inspection Box'. (The 'Our setting's successes' book from the activity 'Maximising strengths' on page 84 would be very suitable!)

➤ Spend approximately 20 minutes reading through all the headings listed on the first and second sheet of paper on the flipchart, outlining how you can cover the requirements and when you will do this by. Complete the chart accordingly.

➤ Look at the third sheet of paper on the flipchart and ask for the staff's ideas for the celebration. Settings need to have something planned for the children and the staff to move on to after inspection, as a step back towards reality! Encourage ideas by outlining possibilities, for example, an educational visit, a

theatre group, an artist or author's visit, a teddy bears' picnic and so on. (In addition, consider a special social event for the staff!)

➤ Go on to the fourth sheet of paper on the flipchart and address the headings. The most important thing is to reassure the staff that they will have done all their preparations by then. They should put all their energies into helping the children make the best possible progress in their learning – and if they do that, the quality of their teaching should be good.

➤ Another key factor will be listening carefully to what the inspectors say and sharing this with the staff. This will enable you to find more evidence, if necessary, for inspectors or demonstrate something that they are looking for in your normal practice. Spend approximately ten minutes on this.

➤ Give a copy of the photocopiable sheet to each member of staff and ask them to go through their checklist, identifying how far they have got with their preparations. Circulate and support individuals.

Further action

➤ Let the staff use their check-lists to work through as they prepare. Have another session ten days before the inspection so that everyone can check and share their planning, making any final adjustments after discussions. Add copies to the 'Inspection documents' file. Collect and add other evidence to the 'Inspection box' and arrange to give all this information to the inspectors.

Post-inspection issues

Look at how everyone can be involved in post-inspection action plans

🏃 Number of staff
All, plus managers and linked governors.

🕐 Timing
1 hour 30 minutes, plus 45 minutes final review session.

What you need
➤ A copy of the photocopiable sheet on page 150 for each member of staff; pens; copy of OFSTED report for each member of staff; feedback notes from lessons or on your provision; flipchart; Blu-Tack; felt-tipped pens; large Post-it notes or similar; highlighter pens.

What you do
➤ Explain that the aim of this session is to involve everyone in creating the post-OFSTED action plan and to work out how to address the inspection findings.
➤ Spend five minutes reading through the first sheet of paper on the flipchart and explaining the requirements and time-scales for your setting.
➤ In schools, explain that your action plan ideas will give you a clear

Preparation
➤ Prepare the flipchart as follows, selecting the appropriate headings:
On a sheet of paper write:
What schools and providers have to do
♦ Schools must send a copy of the 'Summary report' to all parents.
♦ Other providers must make a copy of the report available to all parents.
♦ Within 40 working days of receiving the OFSTED report all providers must prepare an action plan to deal with the key issues identified in the inspection.
♦ Schools must create an action plan, approved by governors. Where there is a key issue for the Foundation Stage, practitioners should feed ideas into this.
♦ In schools, all parents must receive a summary of the action plan.
♦ In other settings, the provider must make a copy of the plan available to all parents and usually to the local education authority (as a condition of registration in the Early Years Development and Childcare Partnership (EYDCP)).

➤ Familiarise yourself with your OFSTED report. Schools should go through the 'How high are standards?'; 'How well are the children taught?' and 'How good are curricular and other opportunities offered to the children?' sections as well as the Foundation stage report, highlighting any pertinent text. Write this on separate sheets of paper on the flipchart.
➤ Study the Foundation Stage section and highlight all the positives in one colour and the negatives in another. Check the 'What the school should do to improve further' section and if there are any key issues that apply to the Foundation Stage, write these out in full on another sheet of paper on the flipchart sheet. Otherwise, list the main areas of weakness from the Foundation paragraphs.
➤ In other settings, read through your report and highlight the positives and negatives in different colours. Write out each 'What the setting needs to do next ' key issue on a separate sheet of paper on the flipchart.

early years
training & management

framework to check your own progress. (In many schools this will form the phase action plan to be managed by the Foundation Stage Co-ordinator.)

➤ Reveal the flipchart comments from different report sections and spend ten minutes discussing these.

➤ Give a copies of the OFSTED report to each member of staff. Spend approximately 20 minutes reading through the different Foundation Stage paragraphs, or the full report for other settings, noting the strengths and weaknesses in each Area of Learning or provision. Use your highlighted copy to draw attention to these.

➤ Refer back to any feedback from the inspectors, giving more examples to support judgements. Then turn to the separate issues for improvement.

➤ Display the separate sheets prominently and discuss these together for ten minutes.

➤ If the staff feel that judgements are harsh or incorrect, stress that you must address the key issues for improvement positively, and that everyone can build on existing good practice. Do not waste energy on denial – move on!

➤ Give a copy of the photocopiable sheet to each member of staff and read through the headings, explaining that these are the areas that OFSTED will expect to see covered. If your setting is unfamiliar with action planning, spend some time going through the format.

➤ Look at your first key issue or weakness. Give out the Post-it notes. Ask the staff to work in pairs, using their photocopiable sheet as a guide.

➤ Invite them to write suggestions for action, when it could be done and who might do it – who might check it is done and how they would know if they are successful. Discuss

possible ideas together. Let the staff stick their completed Post-it notes on to the relevant flipchart sheet.

➤ Use most of the remaining time to repeat the task for all other key issues. Circulate and support the staff, emphasising the need for different ideas for action.

➤ Finally, as a whole group, read through and briefly discuss the different ideas on each Key Issue sheet together. Add any ideas that are sparked off from these.

➤ Explain that you will use these as a starting-point for completing the action plan. Arrange a further session when you can share the draft with staff and agree the final plan.

Further action

➤ Enlarge a copy of the photocopiable sheet to maximum size for each key issue or weakness, and stick the staff's Post-it notes in the appropriate columns. Try to incorporate as many suggestions as possible. If any are unsuitable, see if any elements could be used – if not, put them to one side. Fill in as many of the columns as you can, then copy the sheet out as large as possible.

➤ Hold a second session and display these sheets. Explain that you have tried to include most ideas. Encourage the staff to suggest ways to fill in all missing columns, agreeing the most productive. Stress that staff cannot easily check and lead the same development, so nominate a range of 'monitors'. Ensure that actions are realistically spread over several terms and that resources include staff time and actual costings.

A check-list for your setting concerning the issues raised in **Chapter 6** Inspection issues

➤ Are all the staff familiar with the last inspection report?

➤ Have we taken time to share it together?

➤ Have we fully discussed the implications for our setting?

➤ Have we looked at the whole school 'key issues' that were in the last report and considered how our setting has contributed towards progress in these areas? (Schools.)

➤ Have we familiarised ourselves with the whole of the report, as well as the section on the Foundation Stage provision? (Schools.)

➤ Have we reviewed our last action plan and recorded the progress that we have made?

➤ Have we looked at areas where progress has been more limited and made further plans to begin to tackle these before the inspection?

➤ How have we identified what we think we do well? How have we gathered evidence for this?

➤ Is our evidence strong, well represented, in an accessible format and ready to present to the inspectors?

➤ Have we used this to inform managers, governors, other colleagues and parents who may be involved in the inspection process?

➤ Have we also identified our weaker areas of provision?

➤ Have we taken positive steps towards improving these before the inspection?

➤ How have we gathered evidence?

➤ In what way shall we share this with the inspectors?

➤ Are managers, governors and other colleagues aware of our plans for improvement?

➤ How are we preparing for the inspection visit itself?

➤ Is our setting ready for any pre-inspection visit and tour by the lead inspector? (Schools.)

➤ Have we reviewed and reminded all the staff of our policies and relevant documents?

➤ Are these all collected together and ready for the inspectors?

➤ Are all the children who will 'read' and talk to the inspectors identified and prepared?

➤ Have we assembled a broad range of work, photographs and evidence of children's work for the inspectors?

➤ Have we annotated broad ability bands and other key information on this work? How will this be presented?

➤ Have we agreed our planning for the inspection period?

➤ Has this been checked carefully and are learning objectives clear?

➤ Are all the staff, particularly support staff, clear about what they are to do?

➤ Have we prepared written activity cards for parents and helpers?

➤ Have all the necessary resources been collected?

➤ Are all our displays of high quality and do they represent a broad base of different work?

➤ Is a strong commitment to literacy and numeracy evident in displays?

➤ What strategies have we got in place for 'rainy day' problems?

➤ Have we 'decluttered' everywhere and checked this throughout the setting?

➤ Have we done a health and safety tour to check all the areas?

➤ Do we know how we will share feedback with all the staff?

Staff training activities   early years
**training &
management**

Chapter 7 Equal opportunities, Inclusion, Behaviour and Special needs

Every setting should ensure that all the children, irrespective of their personal backgrounds and circumstances, have equal access to a quality early years provision. This chapter will help you to review your own policies and provision.
The importance of early years education in providing a strong foundation to all other learning is now officially recognised and, indeed, is a key factor in helping young children have equal opportunities and experiences to set them on their learning careers. This chapter aims to help practitioners in all settings rise to the challenge of ensuring that their provision can meet these demands.

Raising staff awareness
The first activity on page 94 focuses on raising the awareness of all staff about equal opportunity issues and explains that this is not optional! In this training unit, due stress is placed on the need for settings to show that they are pro-active and plan to meet the children's diverse needs.

The activity on page 96 focuses on the government emphasis on inclusion and the practical implications for all settings. Training is firmly focused on using your own planning as a starting-point and reviewing your own current practice together – identifying areas that may need more attention.

All practitioners will realise the importance of developing a positive behaviour policy. The activity on page 98 highlights practical ways to review, and then develop, your own setting's approach to this area. Some of the tasks are light-hearted but have a serious message behind them!

Special needs
The training session in the activity on page 100 aims to extend the staff's understanding of the requirements of the revised SEN *Code of Practice*. It breaks down the complexities of the requirements in a simple form to aid busy practitioners in their work. It also enables all settings to consider how they can meet the requirements and what roles staff members and other colleagues and agencies need to play at different times.

The activity on page 102 looks in more detail at how the staff can best help specific children with special educational needs in your particular setting. It gives a vital opportunity for the SENCO to work with all the staff in order to explain Individual Education Plans (IEPs) and the importance of following the plans through.

Working with parents
The final activity on page 104 focuses on the sensitive, and sometimes daunting, area of working with parents and other agencies, as well as record-keeping. Once more the SENCO takes on a prominent role, but tasks are structured to give the staff a clear awareness of their own responsibilities, reminding them that special needs is not only the province of the SENCO!

Equal opportunities audit

Focus on the requirements for an equal opportunities policy

༄ Number of staff
All.

⏱ Timing
Approximately 1 hour.

What you need
A copy of the photocopiable sheet on page 151 for each member of staff; pens; flipchart; felt-tipped pens; copies of any equal opportunities or related policies that you have for each member of staff.

What you do
➤ Explain that the aim of this session is to raise awareness of the requirements for an equal opportunities policy for all settings and to review the effectiveness of your current practice.
➤ Make a strong statement that stresses that equal opportunities is not something that happens by

Preparation
➤ Prepare the flipchart as follows:

Sheet 1
Equal opportunities – meeting the diverse needs of children
♦ Practitioners must be aware of the different experiences, interests, skills and knowledge that affect their ability to learn.
♦ Settings need an understanding of equal opportunities requirements that cover race, gender and disability and the revised SEN *Code of Practice*.
♦ Settings need to review their practice and actively plan to ensure that all the children have equal access to learning.

Sheet 2
Practitioners need to plan to meet the needs of:
♦ boys and girls
♦ children with special educational needs
♦ children who are more able
♦ children with disabilities
♦ children from all social, cultural and religious backgrounds
♦ children from different ethnic groups (including Travellers, refugees and asylum seekers)
♦ children from diverse linguistic backgrounds.

Sheets 3 and 4
'In order to meet children's diverse needs, and

help all children make the best possible progress, practitioners should:
♦ PLAN opportunities that build on and extend children's knowledge, experiences, interests and skills and develop their self-esteem and confidence in their ability to learn
♦ USE a wide range of teaching strategies based on children's learning needs
♦ PROVIDE a wide range of opportunities to motivate, support and develop children and help them to be involved, concentrate and learn effectively
♦ PROVIDE a safe and supportive learning environment, free from harassment, in which the contribution of children is valued and where racial, religious, disability and gender stereotypes are challenged
♦ USE materials that positively reflect diversity and are free from discrimination and stereotyping
♦ PLAN challenging opportunities for children whose ability and understanding are in advance of their language and communication skills
♦ MONITOR children's progress, identifying any areas of concern, and taking action to provide support, for example, by using different approaches, additional adult help or other agencies'.
(Taken from the *Curriculum Guidance for the Foundation Stage* (QCA)).

accident and that even if your practice is good, you need to ensure that your setting is pro-active in promoting it. OFSTED inspectors will judge the impact of the way that each setting actively takes steps to implement equal opportunities.

➤ Give out copies of your equal opportunities policy to each member of staff. Spend approximately ten minutes going through this together to remind the staff of your stance.

➤ Look at the first sheet of paper on the flipchart and spend five minutes reading through the headings. Explain that these points are not optional but are the expected requirements of all settings. Ascertain whether the staff are aware of the legal requirements of the second bullet point. If not, take steps to obtain the following documents for later reference: The Sex Discrimination Act 1975; The Race Relations Act 1976; The Disability Discrimination Act 1995 and the SEN *Code of Practice* 2001 (effective from 1 January 2002).

➤ Move on to the second sheet of paper on the flipchart and work through the list of different categories for approximately ten minutes. Discuss the children in your setting in each group – noting the number, the nature of their diversity and the general context of your setting.

➤ Make a strong point to the staff that, although your setting may not currently have any children from a particular group, for example, children whose mother tongue is not English, your equal opportunities policy needs to recognise their needs. Stress to them that just because you do not currently have representatives of these groups, it does not mean that this will always be the case.

➤ Also stress that even if you have few, if any, children from different ethnic backgrounds, you still have a responsibility to ensure that different cultures, role models and diverse materials are highlighted within your practice. Your children need to have real opportunities to learn about and experience aspects of Britain's rich cultural diversity.

➤ Turn to the third and fourth sheets of paper on the flipchart and explain to the staff that these points are taken from the *Curriculum Guidance for the Foundation Stage* (QCA). Spend ten minutes reading through these headings, discussing each one and giving examples of your own practice.

➤ Now give a copy of the photocopiable sheet to each member of staff and spend a few minutes reading through the checklist headings.

➤ For the remaining time, invite the staff, individually, to complete the sheets, allowing a few minutes at the end of the session to share their thoughts with the whole group.

Further action

➤ Collect in the photocopiable sheets and use these as a review of your provision and the level of your staff's understanding. Arrange follow-up sessions to focus on any aspects that appear thinly covered in your practice. If necessary, update your policy. If your setting has few ethnic minority children or children with special needs or physical disabilities, try to make links with a setting with more diversity. Make arrangements for visits or for visiting staff to lead an information sharing session at your setting.

➤ Compile an 'Equal opportunities guidance file', with different sections for each different need, such as gender. Over a period of time, add examples of good practice, ideas to extend learning, articles and suggestions from publications, reports of visits and specialist visitors. Build up a reference bank to support staff planning.

Inclusion in the curriculum

Concentrate on educational inclusion within your setting

Number of staff
All.

Timing
Approximately 1 hour.

What you need
A copy of the photocopiable sheet on page 152 for each member of staff; pens; paper; flipchart; felt-tipped pens; copies of your next week's planning.

What you do
➤ Explain to the staff that the aim of this session is to ensure that everyone understands what educational inclusion means. Emphasise that it is important that they are fully aware of the implications of this for your setting.

Preparation
➤ Prepare the flipchart as follows:
Sheet 1
What is educational inclusion?
Inclusion means that all children get a fair deal at school or in their settings.
Settings need to try to overcome all possible barriers to learning.
Children need to:
♦ get the best out of their time at our setting, make good progress and learn well
♦ have the opportunity to learn without interference and disruption
♦ have respect and individual help from their teachers and helpers
♦ have access to all aspects of the curriculum
♦ have their well-being and welfare attended to properly
♦ be happy and secure at school.
Sheet 2
What OFSTED inspectors look for:
♦ Do the children achieve as much as they can, according to their individual needs, within the setting?
♦ If not, which groups are not achieving as much as they could, and why?
♦ Is the setting aware of any differences and if not, why not?
♦ How does the setting explain any differences

and are these explanations convincing?
♦ What action has the setting taken to raise standards in underachieving groups and is it appropriate?
♦ What action is the setting taking to promote racial harmony, to prepare the children for living in a diverse and increasingly interdependent society?
♦ What actions does the setting take to prevent and address racism, sexism and other forms of discrimination?
Sheet 3
♦ How well does our setting recognise and take steps to overcome barriers to learning?
♦ Do we know about all the different groups within our own setting?
♦ Do we review how well they all do?
♦ What steps do we take to make sure that particular groups are not disadvantaged in our setting?
♦ What steps do we take to promote their participation and success?
♦ How do we promote good relationships and manage behaviour?
♦ What do we do specifically to prevent and address racism, sexism and other forms of discrimination?
♦ What do we do about it if cases of discrimination occur?

➤ Stress that inclusion is a very strong element of all OFSTED school inspections and has important implications for all settings. Most settings will already address many of the requirements, but will need to check that all areas are given due emphasis.

➤ Ask the staff what they think educational inclusion means. Gather in suggestions for a few minutes and then turn to the first sheet of paper on the flipchart. Explain that these definitions are taken from the OFSTED instructions to inspectors. Read through the headings for a few minutes ensuring that all the staff clearly understand them. Make a positive statement that all the areas should be comfortable for early years practitioners!

➤ Now turn to the second sheet of paper on the flipchart. Explain that these questions are taken from the guidance given to inspectors and make a useful checklist for your own provision. Go through the headings together for approximately ten minutes and stress that the important issue is what a school or setting **actively** does to promote inclusion.

➤ Look at the third sheet of paper on the flipchart. Read through the headings for approximately five minutes. Then ask the staff to work in pairs for another ten minutes, reading through the list and answering the questions and giving examples of good or limited practice. Ask them to make notes of their agreed answers on paper. Spend another five minutes asking each group to feed back on one or two questions of your choice.

➤ Take five minutes to ensure that the staff are aware that promoting inclusion can be done in a number of ways by planning specific activities, selecting appropriate resources, and ensuring that displays, posters, books, dressing-up clothes, artefacts, dolls, home-play materials and so on reflect gender, ability, disability and cultural issues. Promoting inclusion may also mean planning individual support, reviewing the progress of specific groups, and selecting circle time and stories to support good behaviour.

➤ Give a copy of the photocopiable sheet to each member of staff and ask them to look at their next week's planning. Invite them to work in pairs or their normal planning groups. Spend the remaining time working through the photocopiable sheet and noting what action the staff propose to take, with respect to their planned activities and selection of resources, for the following week's work. Circulate and help them to focus on pro-active provision.

➤ Spend a few minutes at the end of the session sharing some of the ideas together and write a list of the most useful ones. Ask the staff to ensure that inclusion issues are considered for all future planning.

Further action

➤ Make copies of the second and third sheets of paper on the flipchart and give these out with the staff's ideas for inclusion planning as a prompt and guide for everyone.

➤ Compile a list of the children and clearly identify the different groups that they may belong to, such as ethnic minority group, ability, specific physical issues, special educational needs and so on. Ensure that all the staff are aware of these children's needs and plan for them accordingly. Be sensitive to the confidential nature of this information.

➤ Arrange another review session later to evaluate your progress and add to the list of good practice. Audit your resources (see the activity 'Auditing your resources' on page 38 and make a list of needs. Plan to fill any gaps by fund-raising or through normal purchasing.

A positive behaviour policy

Consider how to promote good behaviour within your setting

Number of staff
All.

Timing
Two sessions – 1 hour 15 minutes for the first session; 45 minutes for the second session.

What you need
Paper; pens; flipchart; felt-tipped pens; postcards (cut in half); small box; Blu-Tack; carrier bag; sticky tape; copies of your setting's behaviour policy.

What you do

Session 1

➤ Explain to the staff that the aim of this session is to review and develop your setting's approach to promoting good behaviour.

➤ Produce your 'Good behaviour box' and display it prominently. Give out some postcard halves and ask the staff to spend up to ten minutes jotting down one issue per card that helps the children to behave well. When the time is up, put the cards in the box for later use.

➤ Now hold up your 'Bad behaviour bag'. Give out more cards and ask everyone to pretend to be a child and write down any situations or circumstances that might make them behave badly. Spend ten minutes on this task. Collect the cards in the bag and place it to one side.

➤ Look at the first sheet of paper on the flipchart. Ask the staff to draw out a suggestion from the 'Good behaviour box', and read it

Preparation

➤ Label the box 'Good behaviour box' and the carrier bag 'Bad behaviour bag'.

➤ Prepare the flipchart as follows:

Sheet 1
Features that promote good behaviour.

Sheet 2
Children may feel insecure and not know how to behave when...

Sheet 3
Key curriculum points for promoting good behaviour
Personal, social and emotional development
Communication, language and literacy

- Supporting transition between settings.
- Promoting an inclusive ethos.
- Demonstrating how each child is a valued member of the community.
- Helping the children to develop a strong self-image and self-esteem.
- Encouraging an enthusiasm for learning.
- Helping the children to become successful learners.
- Providing opportunities for the children to work and co-operate together.
- Helping the children to listen to each other.
- Encouraging concentration and commitment to their tasks.
- Developing the children's communication skills in a wide variety of situations.
- Providing excellent role models ourselves.
- Sharing stories and books with relevant content.
- Circle time.
- Snack time.

Sheet 4 (leave spaces between the headings)
Key curriculum points for promoting good behaviour
Mathematics
Knowledge and understanding of the world
Physical development
Creative development

out loud. Ask if the staff agree that it promotes good behaviour, saying why they think so. Fix all agreed cards to the chart. Discard any that do not have universal agreement, after discussion. Read through all the suggestions, taking approximately 15 minutes for this section.

➤ Display this chart, then reveal the second sheet of paper on the flipchart. Now produce the 'Bad behaviour bag' and repeat the exercise, this time attaching all the suggestions to the chart. Have some fun and amusement with the comments – but be sure to stress that the children may feel the way that the card implies and practitioners need to think about this. Put the completed chart to one side (ready for later action).

➤ Now turn to the third sheet of paper on the flipchart. Explain that all these key points have been drawn from the *Curriculum Guidance for the Foundation Stage* (QCA) and are curriculum issues that should help to promote good behaviour. Emphasise that behaviour management is not just a set of rules or procedures, although these are important factors. Stress the importance of curriculum opportunities that reinforce positive behaviour and the development of positive attitudes. Spend 20 minutes reading through the headings together. Ask the staff to give examples of how good behaviour could be reinforced through each one.

➤ Turn to the fourth sheet of paper on the flipchart. Give the staff some paper and ask them to work in pairs to suggest positive strategies to build on good behaviour in the other four Areas of Learning. Take 15 minutes for this activity, allowing a few extra minutes for feedback of ideas. Record these on to the sheet.

➤ Finally, take the second sheet of paper on the flipchart and the 'Bad behaviour bag'. Say that you need positive approaches to behaviour management to enable the children to succeed, so negatives should not be allowed! Dramatically screw up the sheet, put it into the 'bag' and bin it!

Session 2

➤ Remind the staff of the work that they did in Session 1 and display the first, third and fourth sheet of paper on the flipchart. Now give copies of your behaviour policy to each member of staff, Read through this together. Ask if the policy covers everything that it should or if it needs updating, amending or adjusting, and if so how.

➤ Spend approximately 20 minutes reading through the policy, making any changes or noting what additional information is needed.

➤ Ask the staff to be clear about the audience for the policy. How will your policy be communicated to parents? Visitors? Governors? Inspectors? Decide whether there need to be slightly different versions. Spend approximately 15 minutes deciding on a version for parents.

➤ For the remaining time of the session, discuss and decide how your policy will be communicated to all those who you feel the need to be aware of it.

Further action

➤ Finalise your policy and any support guidance that you feel would be useful. Put a visitors' or supply staff pack together so that they will quickly be able to understand your approach and any details of what is expected. Design an attractive summary to give to parents and arrange to include this as part of your induction procedures and on your parents' noticeboard.

The SEN Code of Practice

Focus on implementing the SEN Code of Practice and its implications

Number of staff

All, plus managers and SENCOs.

Timing

1 hour 15 minutes.

What you need

A copy of photocopiable sheet on page 153 for each member of staff; pens; flipchart; felt-tipped pens; The Special Educational Needs Code of Practice (available from DfES Publications, PO Box 5050, Sherwood Park, Annesley, Nottinghamshire NG15 0DJ, tel: 0845-6022260) and Section 6 of The SEN Toolkit (available from the same source); copies of pages 15 and 26 (Roles and responsibility tables) of the Code for each person.

Preparation

➤ Prepare the flipchart as follows:

Sheet 1

Principles of the Code of Practice

♦ A child with SEN should have their needs met.

♦ The SEN of children will normally be met in mainstream schools or settings.

♦ The views of the child should be sought and taken into account.

♦ Parents have a vital role in supporting their child's education.

♦ Children with SEN should be offered full access to a broad, balanced and relevant education, including an appropriate curriculum for the Foundation Stage and National Curriculum.

Sheet 2

Critical success factors

♦ The culture, practice, management and deployment of resources in a school or setting are designed to ensure that all the children's need are met.

♦ Local education authorities, schools and settings work together to ensure that the children's SEN are identified early.

♦ Local education authorities, schools and settings exploit best practice when devising interventions.

♦ Account is taken of the wishes of any child in the light of their age and understanding.

♦ Special educational professionals and parents work in partnership.

♦ Parents' views regarding their child's particular needs are taken into account.

♦ Interventions for each child, the impact and child's progress, are reviewed regularly.

♦ There is close co-operation, and a multi-disciplinary approach, with all agencies.

♦ Local education authorities make assessments within prescribed time limits.

♦ Where local education authorities agree statements, they are clear and detailed.

Sheet 3

Early Years Action

When practitioners or the SENCO identify a child with SEN they should devise interventions that are additional or different from part of your usual curriculum.

Triggers – when the child:

♦ makes little or no progress despite targeted approaches

♦ continues to work at levels below those expected for their age

♦ has persistent emotional and/or behavioural problems not ameliorated by your approaches

♦ has sensory/physical problems and makes poor progress despite special aids

♦ has communication problems and requires individual intervention to learn.

Sheet 4
Early Years Action Plus
This is characterised by the involvement of external support agencies who help settings with advice on Individual Education Plans (IEPs) and targets, provide more specialist assessments and may give extra support. The kinds of advice and support will vary according to local policies.
Triggers – when a child:
♦ makes little or no progress over a long period
♦ works at a level substantially below that expected for their age
♦ has emotional/behavioural difficulties that substantially interfere with their own and others learning, despite help
♦ has sensory/physical needs requiring help from a specialist service
♦ has communication difficulties that form substantial barriers to learning.

What you do
➤ Explain that the aim of this session is to help raise awareness of the implications of the revised *Code of Practice* for your setting.
➤ Show the staff the *Code* and the *Toolkit* and stress that although the *Code* is a complex requirement and should be used for reference, the principles and outlines are somewhat simpler to digest.
➤ Spend approximately ten minutes reading through the headings on the first sheet of paper on the flipchart together, encouraging staff discussion on each point.
➤ Now share the second sheet of paper on the flipchart. Spend another 15 minutes reading through these points, seeking staff opinions and comments and discussing possible approaches for your setting.
➤ Reveal the third sheet of paper on the flipchart. Explain that 'Early Years Action' (or 'School Action') is the additional support that you give to a child who you feel has SEN, within your own organisation and resources. Spend five minutes reading through the triggers, then display the sheet prominently, moving on to the fourth sheet of paper on the flipchart. Read through these definitions and triggers for a further five minutes.
➤ Give a copy of the photocopiable sheet to each member of staff and look at the headings together. Spend five minutes talking about the different roles that the people listed on the sheet may have in your setting. Now distribute the photocopied tables from the *Code*.
➤ For 15 minutes, ask the staff to work in pairs, using the tables to complete their photocopiable sheets. Let one half of the group work on 'Early Years Action' and the other on 'Early Years Action Plus'.
➤ For the remaining time, let each pair feed back their ideas. Discuss and agree the different roles and responsibilities in your setting.

Further action
➤ Draw up a clear table for 'Early Years Action' and 'Early Years Action Plus' that shows all the roles and responsibilities of each staff member. For example, 'Support staff discuss concerns with key staff (named)', 'School SENCO asked to visit and give advice in nursery' or 'Manager arranges annual review of SEN policy'. Circulate the table to all the staff and display an enlarged copy in the staff room. Also share an outline of this at parents' and governors' meetings.

Supporting children with SEN

Consider ways to meet the requirements of children with special needs

⚞ Number of staff
All, plus managers and SENCOs.

⏲ Timing
1 hour.

What you need
A copy of the photocopiable sheet on page 154 for each member of staff; pens; SENCO records; copies of IEPs for the children in your setting for each member of staff; flipchart; felt-tipped pens.

What you do
➤ Explain that the aim of this session is to look at how your setting focuses its work to meet the needs of the children at the 'Early Years Action' stage of support. If necessary, remind the staff of the differences and triggers for 'Early Years Action' and 'Early Years Action Plus'.
➤ Make a strong statement about the importance of early identification of SEN based on very careful observation and record-keeping. Stress the need for real evidence on the children with SEN, particularly to feed into reviews with parents and if a child needs to go forward for

Preparation
➤ It would be useful to have undertaken the activity 'The SEN *Code of Practice* on page 100 before carrying out this unit.
➤ Discuss the children that have SEN in your setting with your SENCO and decide on one or two different children who information could be used for this activity. Prepare the information (gather records of observations, details of reviews, parents' comments and so on to share with staff). Ask the SENCO to prepare a 'thumbnail sketch' of each chosen child and be ready to lead discussions on what action has been taken. Make a large copy of each child's Individual Education Plan (IEP). If possible, select one child with 'Early Years Action' and one with 'Early Years Action Plus'.
➤ If you currently have no identified children with SEN, arrange for a SENCO for another setting to visit you and follow the above preparations. Your teacher-mentor will be able to suggest a good source.

➤ Prepare the flipchart as follows:
Sheet 1
Action to meet SEN
♦ The key test of the need for further action is evidence that the current rate of progress is inadequate.
♦ There should not be an assumption that all pupils will progress at the same rate.
♦ Children must not be regarded as having a learning difficulty solely because the language, or forms of language, of their home is different from the language in which they will be taught.
Sheet 2
Relating intervention to individual needs
♦ Decisions about which actions are appropriate for which the children must be made on an individual basis –
by a careful assessment of the children's difficulties, the children's need for different approaches to learning and the school and classroom context.

support from other agencies and 'Early Years Action Plus'.

➤ Show the first sheet of paper on the flipchart and spend a few minutes reading through the points, emphasising that these are quoted from the SEN *Code of Practice*. Encourage staff comments.

➤ Move on to the second sheet of paper on the flipchart. Read through the headings together and emphasise the individual nature of the children and their learning difficulties, and emphasise that this needs a tailored response from the setting.

➤ Now introduce your SENCO (or visiting SENCO). Highlight the confidential nature of any shared information, particularly if you have a visiting SENCO. Ask them to give a case history of one child – from early concerns and eventual identification to meeting their needs in the setting. Ask the SENCO to share sensitively the processes of involving parents – engaging their support and obtaining their views, possibly eliciting the child's views (if appropriate) and the need for termly review. Spend approximately 15 minutes on this presentation.

➤ Encourage the staff to contribute where they have been involved in the process or to ask questions.

➤ Repeat with detailed discussions about another child with different needs, taking ten minutes overall.

➤ Give a copy of the photocopiable sheets to each member of staff. Tell them the name of a specific child and display the enlarged version of their IEP. Let the SENCO go through the various sections and explain the content.

➤ Now ask the staff to work in pairs. Invite them to use the information from the IEP to swiftly complete the top half of the sheet

and any reference to parents'/child's views at the bottom.

➤ Then ask them to discuss ways to plan to meet the needs of this child. Encourage them to consider the activities that they would plan and how these would be organised; how staff might be deployed to give special targeted support; what special resources might need to be made or obtained, plus any other features of appropriate action. Let them complete this section on the sheet.

➤ Invite the staff to complete the next section and write in forms of observation and other evidence that would be useful to check the child's progress or to pass on – if necessary – to other agencies. Allow 20 minutes in total for completing the sheet.

➤ For the remaining time, share each pair's ideas with the whole group.

Further action

➤ Arrange a session after each termly review of the children with SEN, so that information can be shared and all the staff are clear as to the new targets for each child. Ask the staff to suggest ideas as to how each child can be supported and agree what evidence will be required, and who will gather it.

➤ Organise a visit to another setting and discuss the nature of their children with SEN. Observe how they support them. Develop a database of contacts for voluntary agencies and specialist support for future reference.

Working with other parties

Concentrate on a partnership approach when supporting children with SEN

⚇ Number of staff

All, including SENCOs.

⏱ Timing

1 hour.

What you need

A copy of the photocopiable sheet on page 155 for each member of staff; pens; enlarged copy of the photocopiable sheet; flipchart; felt-tipped pens; the SEN *Code of Practice* and Section 6 of the SEN *Toolkit*; SENCO records/IEPs on specific children.

What you do

➤ Explain that the aims of this session are to highlight the need for a partnership approach to providing support for the children with SEN, and for the staff to understand the importance of keeping records which detail the progress of a child with identified SEN. (These aims are vital in monitoring progress, when moving a child from 'Early Years Action' to 'Early Years Action Plus',

Preparation

➤ Familiarise yourself with the revised SEN *Code of Practice*, particularly Chapter 2 – 'Working in partnership with parents'. If possible, undertake the activities 'The SEN *Code of Practice*' on page 100 and 'Supporting children with SEN' on page 102 before carrying out this session.

➤ Discuss this session with the SENCO and decide which child's information will be used, or consult your Teacher Mentor or colleagues and obtain some anonymous examples.

Sheet 1

Strands of action to meet SEN

Action to meet children's SEN tends to fall within four broad bands:

Assessment, planning and review – a cycle

♦ Assessment of a child's rate of progress, specific difficulties and needs.

♦ What will be planned to help the child make progress.

♦ Review at regular intervals to see how successfully support is working.

Grouping for teaching purposes

♦ Considering how the child will be taught at different times and who will do this.

♦ Allocating a key member of staff to ensure continuity and security.

Additional human resources

♦ Deploying your own staff to meet the child's needs best.

♦ Involving support staff.

♦ Involving parents, helpers and so on, plus specialist advisers.

Curriculum and teaching methods

♦ Working out the best strategies and support for a child's learning.

♦ Making adaptations to the usual programme to meet the child's needs.

♦ Adapting teaching approaches to help the child make maximum progress.

Sheet 2

Partnership with parents

♦ The school or setting is often the first point of contact for parents.

♦ Parents need to feel welcomed and valued.

♦ Parents need to be informed sensitively if their child may have SEN.

♦ Parents should be involved in helping their child, and settings should help them know what to do at home.

♦ Parents need to know what the setting is doing to help their child (interventions).

♦ Parents need to feed information into their child's progress profile and be involved in regular reviews.

Sheet 3

Individual records for children with SEN.

In addition to the standard setting records, children with identified SEN need extra information in their profiles.

Records should include:

♦ progress (dated reviews)

♦ behaviour and attitudes

♦ support strategies (and their impact)

♦ information from parents (regularly updated)

♦ information from health, social services or other agencies

♦ the child's own perceptions of difficulties (if appropriate).

and when securing additional help from specialist agencies.)

➤ Display the first sheet of paper on the flipchart and spend ten minutes reading through the 'Strands of action'. Explain that these are taken from the *Code of Practice* and are the expected areas of action to be followed when supporting children with SEN. If possible, ask the staff to give real examples.

➤ Move on to the second sheet of paper on the flipchart. Remind the staff that the *Code* emphasises the joint setting/parental approach. Settings are expected to develop strong parental partnerships but parents are also expected to play their part responsibly (pages 17–18 in the *Code* – that provide useful quotes for school and setting SEN policies). Spend five minutes reading through the sheet explaining that these points are embedded in the *Code of Practice*.

➤ Look at the third sheet of paper on the flipchart and then spend a few minutes reading through the expectations regarding records for children with SEN (see page 35 of the *Code* – 'Individual records').

➤ Now ask the SENCO to present information on one child in your setting (or an anonymous case study). Take approximately 15 minutes for this task and encourage the staff to ask questions or seek clarifications.

➤ Present the enlarged photocopiable sheet. Explain that this is a 'prompt sheet' for the staff when discussing a child's progress with parents or other agencies. Spend approximately five minutes discussing the top section of the details and the first layer of columns on the photocopiable sheet. Talk about what assessment happened, what planning was agreed, how this was reviewed and what further action the group might suggest to be discussed at a review meeting.

➤ Give a copy of the photocopiable sheet to each member of staff and then ask them to work in pairs using the case history to complete the rest of the sheet in 15 minutes, particularly considering how they would make sensitive suggestions for further action. Circulate, with the SENCO, to give support to the staff.

➤ For the remaining time, invite each group to feed back their ideas. Ask how they would tackle aggressive or unrealistic views and encourage parents to help at home.

Further action

➤ Prepare supportive 'How can I help?' parental booklets, tailor-made for each child with SEN. Develop a bank of 'activity kits' that can be sent home for parents to use.

➤ Develop an attractive 'user-friendly' page for parents to use as their own prompt sheet for reviews.

A check-list for your setting concerning the issues raised in **Chapter 7** Equal opportunities, Inclusion, Behaviour and Special needs

➤ What is the staff's level of awareness of equal opportunity issues?

➤ Do we have a policy that covers all the areas we need to?

➤ Does our policy cover how we plan to meet the needs of boys and girls?

➤ Does it cover our approach to the children with special educational needs?

➤ Is the policy clear about meeting the needs of more able children?

➤ Does it address the needs of the children with disabilities?

➤ Does it include specific reference to children from different social, cultural and religious backgrounds and our response to their needs?

➤ Even if we have few, if any, children from different ethnic groups, does our policy indicate what our approach would be should some join our setting – or how our provision would reflect this?

➤ Does it address the issues for the children of diverse linguistic backgrounds?

➤ How does our practice measure up to our policy?

➤ What evidence is there for how we meet, or would meet, the needs of these different groups?

➤ Do our resources (books, materials, dressing up clothes, home-play equipment, pictures, artefacts, toys, small-world items and so on) reflect the diverse needs of the children from many backgrounds and circumstances?

➤ Do we review the progress carefully of the children from different backgrounds and circumstances? How well do they do?

➤ What positive actions do we take to encourage their progress?

➤ How do we avoid deliberate or unwitting discrimination?

➤ How do we ensure that all the staff act consistently?

➤ How do we ensure that supply staff, helpers and visitors also carry out our policy?

➤ How effective is our behaviour policy in practice?

➤ Is this shared clearly with parents regularly?

➤ Do we monitor behaviour and spend time regularly to discuss a unified approach?

➤ Are we familiar with the SEN *Code of Practice?*

➤ Have we adopted this in our setting?

➤ How do we carry out 'Early Years Action'?

➤ What happens for 'Early Years Action Plus' in our setting?

➤ Which children have SEN?

➤ How are the new children identified?

➤ What is the SENCO's role?

➤ Do the staff understand their own responsibilities for supporting the children with SEN?

➤ How do we know how well our children with SEN are progressing?

➤ Do we spend time discussing specific children with SEN and adapt our programmes accordingly?

➤ Who contributes to the assessment and recording progress?

➤ Which other agencies does the setting work with?

➤ How are different staff involved with other agencies?

➤ Do we have a consistent approach when working with parents of children with SEN? How do we ensure this?

➤ Do we discuss how to deal with sensitive issues?

Chapter 8 Staff development

Staff development is a vital tool to keep everyone fresh and motivated and to share ideas. Use the suggestions in this chapter to keep your staff up to date with training and to consider new developments in early years' education.

It is important to plan time for all the staff to consider different approaches and to reflect on their own practice. The most effective settings plan regular training sessions as part of their staff meeting schedules. OFSTED inspectors will look to see how much training has been undertaken and how any setting seeks to address staff development over a period of time.

Appraisal and review

This chapter covers many issues concerning staff development and is a useful starting-point for several important elements of any setting's programme. The first activity on page 108 concentrates on the potentially sensitive issues of appraisal and review, highlighting the very positive outcomes of establishing a regular cycle for all the staff, whatever their role. This training session should help settings to create their own programme or may help a setting to build on its current practice in a beneficial way.

The training unit in the activity on page 110 helps settings to examine the merits, and possible disadvantages, of establishing a performance-management system for all the staff. The adoption of such a scheme, adapted to your setting's unique circumstances, can be a very

powerful tool in maintaining momentum and sustaining high standards and improvement.

Identifying skills

The activity on page 112 is designed to identify the wide range of skills that the staff members of any setting will have, and which are frequently under-used – or sometimes not known about! This training session should be a confidence booster to all staff and should provide some exciting new ideas for inclusion in your provision.

All settings need to have opportunities for team building, not just when new staff are involved, but also to rejuvenate more established teams. The activity on page 114 enables the staff to highlight the key elements of successful teamwork, recognise the negative hindrances and plan further action in an unthreatening way. This unit also includes a fun way to value all staff as individuals and boost confidence!

In the activity on page 116, the focus is on developing a structure for your setting that imbeds positive staff development strategies. This will ensure that all the staff can have access to the type of development they need – addressing the balance of both their personal development and the overall setting.

Finally, the activity on page 119 helps the staff to look at how sharing roles and delegating specific responsibilities can be most effectively carried out. It is designed to help both the manager or delegating member of staff, and those who are to undertake the task.

Appraisal and review

Focus on establishing an appraisal and review system for your setting

Number of staff
All.

Timing
Approximately 1 hour, plus later individual staff interviews of 45 minutes each.

What you need
A copy of the photocopiable sheet on page 156 for each member of staff, plus an enlarged copy; pens; different-coloured felt-tipped pens; flipchart.

What you do
➤ Explain that the aim of this session is to develop an appraisal and review system for your setting.
➤ Reveal the first sheet of paper on the flipchart and make a positive statement that most successful settings have their own appraisal procedures in place that helps them to develop individual staff and strengthen the team approach.

Preparation
➤ Prepare the enlarged copy of the photocopiable sheet for a 'mythical' member of staff. The entries can be amusing but should generally be plausible and pertinent to your setting, for example:

Joanna Bloggs   Nursery nurse
Specific roles and responsibilities:
◆ Group leader for ten children (three- and four-year-olds).
◆ Joint planning with teacher, responsible for home-group sessions in Communication, language and literacy, Mathematical development, Circle time, Story time and Outdoor-play activities – plus agreed support during general activity times.
◆ First aid.
◆ Parents' group each Thursday (Toddlers' club).
◆ Organising snack time on Tuesdays and Fridays.
◆ Setting up role play area, as agreed.
Successful this year
◆ Setting up the Toddlers' club. Organising activities and helping parents get involved in play with their children because... this was a new venture and very few of the parents knew each other. Now they look forward to the session and seem to trust me.

◆ Setting up the garden centre role-play area because... the children worked well here and became involved for long periods, taking delight in growing things and learning well in Knowledge and understanding of the world. I am especially proud of... the way I dealt with an aggressive parent because... I was nervous but able to calm things down. Later she helped in our setting.
Unsuccessful... The outdoor play area because... we don't have enough ideas or equipment to use in inclement weather.
Next year... I want to develop winter outdoor-play activities more.
Manager's help... Buy a stock of cagoules, wellies and so on for wet-weather play.
◆ Would like some training in SEN support.
➤ Prepare the flipchart with the following:
Sheet 1
The benefits of appraisal
Appraisal should:
◆ be a positive and productive experience for the whole team
◆ value all the staff whatever their roles and responsibilities
◆ give all the staff recognition for their personal contributions
◆ give all the staff the opportunity to discuss their work individually and privately

♦ give all staff time to reflect on what they do well
♦ give all the staff time to consider what further involvement or training they would like
♦ help a setting plan future training needs
Sheet 2 (leave spaces between headings for comments)
The appraisal and review cycle
♦ We need to develop a regular annual cycle.
♦ We need to decide who will be appraised.
♦ We need to decide who will appraise which staff.
♦ We need to decide when it will be carried out.
♦ We need to decide how it will be done.
♦ We need to decide what happens to the information.

➤ Spend approximately five minutes reading through the headings. Stress to the staff that appraisal gives everyone a chance to have time for themselves and their own personal development – a rarity for most busy practitioners!
➤ Turn to the second sheet of paper on the flipchart. Plan to take approximately 20 minutes for this task. Read through all the headings together and then return to each one in turn.
➤ Ask the staff to give suggestions as to how the points could be addressed. For example, the most usual cycle is one year. Very large settings might opt for a two-year cycle, with full appraisal one year, and a shorter review the next.
➤ Explain that in schools, all teachers will be subject to 'Performance management reviews' following the national legislation. However, non-teaching staff are not covered by this requirement and many schools run a parallel appraisal system for the staff.
➤ Point out that the staff could choose to have all appraisals carried out at the same time of year, in the same term, or even spread out over the whole year. This will depend on how many people will appraise and be appraised.

➤ Discuss all the headings thoroughly and write down the final decisions of the group. Decide on a start date for the process and a review date to evaluate how successful the first cycle has been.
➤ Display the 'mythical' staff sheet. Spend ten minutes sharing this example.
➤ Give a copy of the photocopiable sheet to each member of staff and, for the remaining time, ask them to complete these individually. Retain them for their 45 minute appraisal interviews. Stress that all the information will be confidential, except sections 4 and 5.

Further action

➤ Set up and circulate the dates for appraisal as agreed. Start the process with volunteers. Hold a follow-up session for any agreed 'appraisers' and stress that they should use the completed sheets as an agenda, with the staff expanding on their comments.
➤ Spend 45 minutes for each appraisal. Aim for the conversation to be 20 per cent appraiser and per cent appraisee. Reaffirm the confidential nature of this process – although requests from sections 4 and 5 need passing on to the setting manager, who should use the information to support staff (if necessary discussing the issues further, in confidence). Appraisers and appraisees keep the only copies of the sheet.

Performance management

Explore the elements of Performance management within your setting

✹ Number of staff
All.

⏱ Timing
Approximately 1 hour.

What you need
A copy of the photocopiable sheet on page 110 for each member of staff; pens; flipchart; different coloured felt-tipped pens; Post-it notes.

What you do
➤ Explain that the aim of this session is to extend staff understanding of Performance management and to decide whether or not to introduce this, or develop it, for all the staff in your setting
➤ Take approximately 25 minutes to

Preparation
➤ This will depend on the type of setting that you are. If you are a school setting, teacher will already be familiar with the Performance management process, but other staff may not be involved or have any knowledge. Other settings are not subject to Performance management, although some have chosen to be. You will nee to adapt this unit to match the experiences of your staff – or you may prefer to use all the materials as these will usefully reinforce your own practices.
➤ Prepare the flipchart as follows:

Sheet 1
Performance management
♦ This system is a development of appraisal systems but with a whole-setting approach, as well as a focus on individual professional development.
♦ This is a system that enables the staff to have an individual and comprehensive annual review of their work and the contribution that they make to the overall development and success of a setting.

Sheet 2
Performance management focuses on specific areas
♦ How a practitioner plays their part to ensure that the children make good progress in certain aspects (usually linked to whole-setting targets).
♦ How a practitioner contributes to the

overall development of the setting (personal responsibilities).
♦ Personal development pertinent to a practitioner.

Sheet 3
Evaluation of individual performance
♦ Annually, the staff have discussions and a work review with a 'team leader' (generally the colleague who manages their phase group). A team leader should not have more than four colleagues to review.
♦ In addition, at least one lesson or activity is observed – this is known in advance and agreed – with follow-up discussions.
♦ Past work is reviewed and targets are set for the following year (usually one for supporting the children's progress; one for personal contribution and one for professional development, such as training).

Sheet 4
Evaluation of individual performance
♦ Where further training or support is requested by practitioners, to help them meet the particular targets, settings should seek to provide this.
♦ The process, similar to appraisal, is confidential to team leaders and their reviewed colleagues except that aggregated anonymous targets or INSET needs are shared with managers/headteachers and governors to keep them informed of school progress and to help them arrange/budget for training.

♦ In schools, headteachers are also subject to Performance management (with an independent external adviser and governor representatives).

Sheet 5
Is it for us?
Pros and Cons.
♦ Divide the sheet into two columns for staff contributions.

read through the first four sheets on the flipchart. Reveal the first sheet of paper on the flipchart and discuss the headings together. If you are a school, or a setting that has already adopted Performance management, remind the staff of how long this has been in place and who is currently involved. Explain that the statutory requirement only applies to teachers but that many settings and schools have extended this system beneficially to all the staff – who after all, are part of the same team!

➤ Continue familiarising the staff with the process by sharing sheets the second and third sheets of paper on the flipchart. Explain that the process can be valuable to help everyone focus on a setting's agreed areas for development. For example, if a setting is working on improving their Physical development Area of Learning, every member of staff identifies how their work will support the children's progress in this aspect, depending on their actual role in the setting.

➤ Allow time for discussion and questions that might arise. Stress that no one is punished for not reaching targets! However, a focused approach, shared by everyone, can help the team to move forward together and helps people to prioritise their work.

➤ If your setting already has experience of Performance management, talk about your current systems. Encourage the staff to make suggestions for

improvement and talk about what works well. Particularly reassure any staff who are new to this.

➤ Give each member of staff a copy of the photocopiable sheet and read through the headings. Ask them to complete the sheet carefully. Explain that they are to work individually to reflect on the issues, completing the task in approximately 15 minutes, ready to feed back ideas.

➤ Look at the fifth sheet of paper on the flipchart and give out the Post-it notes. Ask the staff to write down their ideas and stick these in either the 'Pro' or 'Con' column. Discuss the results for approximately 15 minutes. Then revisit the 'Con' column and see if these could be turned into positives if certain actions or assurances were planned. If so, write these in a different colour on the chart.

➤ Look at the overall results and discuss how to adopt or develop Performance management. Agree start dates and arrange a follow-up session to present the fine detail.

Further action
➤ Use the results to plan out how many of the Performance management elements your setting will adopt. Decide how many 'team leaders' you will need and arrange visits for them to talk to experienced team leaders in other settings. Ask your teacher-mentor or local education authority for suitable links. If you are a small setting you might cover all the observations and discussions personally, or you could train a team leader support staff member to do this for similar colleagues.

Using staff skills fully

Use your staff's individual skills and experiences to benefit your setting

⁂ Number of staff
All.

⏰ Timing
45 minutes.

What you need
A copy of the photocopiable sheet on page 158 for each member of staff; pens; flipchart; paper; different-coloured felt-tipped pens; masking tape.

Preparation
➤ Prepare the flipchart as follows.

Sheet 1
What is our setting's greatest resource?
Our staff – and the rich and unique skills, talents and experience they bring to our provision!
(Mask the answer with a paper cover fixed with masking tape.)

Sheet 2
What useful experiences have we had?

Sheet 3
What skills and interests do we have?
Outside interests
Skills

Sheet 4
Things we would like to be involved in
♦ In our setting.
♦ Finding out about.
♦ Making visits or links.

What you do
➤ Show the staff the first sheet of paper on the flipchart. Ask them the question and receive all answers enthusiastically. Continue to collect answers, even if someone immediately offers the answer that you will reveal, because it is good to generate positive feelings about your setting.
➤ Remove the paper shield and reveal your answer. Explain that the aim of this session is to identify, share and celebrate people's individual skills, interests and experience, and to see how these could add something special to your setting.
➤ Give each member of staff a copy of the photocopiable sheet and briefly go through the sections together. Explain that you want the staff to reflect before answering, and that they must throw modesty out of the window!
➤ Say that the interests and skills do not need to be ones that have been recognised widely, nor do the staff have to be acknowledged experts!
➤ Also stress that everyone has an opportunity to think about things that they would personally like to lead, or be involved in developing, in the setting. This could be a small idea, such as a new local visit, or a new development such as setting up a website.
➤ Ask the staff to reflect on previous experiences at other settings, during training or from visits that they have made. These can form a source of ideas to build on individually or with other members of the team.
➤ Now ask the staff to complete their own photocopiable sheet, taking approximately ten minutes to do so. Circulate and prompt the staff if you know of a skill they have – most people are very modest. For example, if you know that someone was good at making costumes or has spoken about an outside interest, gently remind them and encourage them to write it down.

➤ Call the group back together and reveal the second sheet of paper on the flipchart. Ask them to recall any positive experience and write this on the chart.

➤ Now ask the staff to take turns to share their responses to the top three sections of their sheet. Spend approximately 15 minutes on this activity. Encourage the staff to take turns to act as scribe and list these on the third sheet of paper on the flipchart. Where more than one member of staff has similar skills or interests, mark these with matching coloured asterisks.

➤ Present the fourth sheet of paper on the flipchart and ask the staff to report back individually on the bottom two sections of their personal copy of the photocopiable sheet. As before, make a record on the chart in the appropriate column, again linking similar ideas together. Take approximately ten minutes to complete this task.

➤ For the remaining time in the session, read through the final lists and decide if there are any projects or ideas that could be further explored or planned into future work.

➤ Agree these and then try to allocate something for each member of staff, either individually or in a group. These could be small projects, such as developing a creative activity using someone's interest in a craft, or bigger scale ventures, such as developing a sensory garden area requiring fund-raising for plants and resources.

➤ Agree time-scales and start times or arrange further group meetings to start the planning process. Work out which things can be started easily and which projects will need longer discussion and gradual implementation.

➤ Finally, collect the staff's photocopiable sheets to keep as a record and focus of any future staff development discussions (or for appraisal or Performance management).

Further action

➤ Draw up a grid with four columns. List all the staff's names in the first column, and agreed actions and ideas in the second column. Add the possible time-scales in the third and 'Further action/research' in the last one. Plan a programme of how ideas can be put into action and circulate this to all the staff.

➤ Make arrangements for requested visits or further research. Encourage the staff to visit libraries and locate useful reading material for any of the projects. Build up a staff reference library of useful publications.

➤ Visits may need to be planned over a long period, because of making necessary links or due to organisational issues in your setting. (You may need to consult your teacher-mentor, or local education authority, to find out where to visit for specific areas to be researched.) To ensure that no member of staff is disappointed, keep everyone informed of what is going on. Even if they may have to wait some time for a request to be realised, the staff will feel valued if you have followed their ideas up.

➤ Ensure that you check how everyone's allocated project is going. Ask the staff how they felt things went and be sure to praise and celebrate all the successes – whether great or small!

Team building

Concentrate on the importance of good staff teamwork

🪆 Number of staff
All.

🕐 Timing
Approximately 1 hour.

What you need

A flipchart; black, red and blue felt-tipped pens; sheets of paper; paper slips; pens; two envelopes for each member of staff; small pieces of card or postcards (enough for twice the number of staff present for each person); two different-coloured packs of Post-it notes (or similar).

Preparation

➤ Write the name of each member of staff on two of the envelopes. On slips of paper, write the name of each member of staff. Batch the postcards together in piles ready for distribution.
➤ Prepare the flipchart as follows using black felt-tipped pen:
Sheet 1
What makes for good teamwork?
Sheet 2
What gets in the way of good teamwork?
Sheet 3
New Year's resolutions.
Sheet 4
Animal.
Instrument.
Magic gift.

What you do

➤ Explain that the aim of this session is to reaffirm the importance of good teamwork and to give your own approach a health check.
➤ Reveal the first sheet of paper on the flipchart and give out several Post-it notes of one colour to each member of staff. Ask them to spend five minutes writing separate ideas of what makes teams work successfully together on their Post-it notes. Attach the Post-it notes to the flipchart.
➤ Spend a further five minutes going through the resulting suggestions and ask the staff for examples of where these have worked well for your team. Put a large red circle around all those Post-it notes that you can give a relevant example to. Draw a blue square around any that a real example cannot be given for.
➤ Turn to the second sheet of paper on the flipchart and give out the second colour of Post-it notes. Repeat the activity, asking the staff to think of all constraints to working well in a team, spending approximately five minutes as before. Encourage them to give general suggestions but also to be honest about constraints in your own circumstances, too.
➤ For a further five minutes, read through the resulting list together, discussing the suggestions. Where the staff can give an example of how any of their suggestions might be true (wholly or partially) for your setting, draw a blue square around the Post-it note. Where the Post-it notes are definitely not applicable to your setting, draw a red circle around them.
➤ Display both sheets of paper where all the staff can see them clearly. Look at all the red circles on the charts and congratulate everyone for their successful team working. Stress that even the best of teams

should review their approach and tackle any areas that need revitalisation.

➤ Now reveal the third sheet of paper on the flipchart. Say that a 'New Year' can actually start at any time that you decide and so can 'Resolutions'! Now look at all the blue square Post-it notes that you have marked on both sheets. Take each one in turn and ask the staff to suggest how these could be turned into red circle positives. For example, if someone has suggested 'Too little time for planning', ask for ideas for minimising the problem. Spend approximately ten minutes taking these suggestions and composing them into 'resolutions' for improved teamwork in your setting. Agree a start date in the immediate future.

➤ Now give out the paper slips. Turn to the fourth sheet of paper on the flipchart. Explain to the staff that everyone will receive a slip of paper with the name of a colleague on it. Each member of staff is to consider their allocated colleague and think of an animal and musical instrument for that person to be should they be transformed! They must also consider some positive reasons for their choice! For example, you may choose a clarinet for a colleague to be because they are versatile and can 'play' or do a great range of things.

➤ Next, ask the staff to choose a 'magic gift' for their allocated colleague. This could be, for example, the chance for them to do something you know that they have always longed to do. Give everyone five minutes to complete their photocopiable sheets.

➤ Let each member of staff read out their colleague's name and their animal, instrument and magic gift – giving the positive reasons. Take enough time for everyone to report.

➤ Finally, give each member of staff their batch of postcards. Arrange the named envelopes on a handy surface to one side of the group. Now ask each person to take two of their postcards for each of their colleagues. On one card, ask them to write a personal quality that they admire about them. This could be related to a real situation, such as 'I appreciated the way that you were so kind to me when I was worried about my family'. On the second card, let them write a professional quality that they admire in that person, for example, 'I admire the skilful way you deal with children whose behaviour is not acceptable'.

➤ As the staff complete their cards, let everyone put them in the correct envelope. When all the cards are completed, give each member of staff their own envelope to take home for them to enjoy reading about how much they are valued by the rest of the team.

Further action

➤ Look carefully at the results of the 'New Year's resolutions' task and consider how you can refine your setting's practice to take account of staff suggestions. After the review, hold another session to share how you can adopt the ideas that were put forward. If there are logistical issues to resolve, ask the team to discuss how these can be sorted out together.

Developing staff profiles

Consider establishing a system to review staff development procedures

⁂ Number of staff
All.

⊙ Timing
1 hour.

What you need
A copy of the photocopiable sheet on page 159 for each member of staff; pens; flipchart; different coloured felt-tipped pens; your setting's post-OFSTED action plan or list of priority areas for development.

What you do
➤ Explain that the aim of this session is to review your staff development procedures and establish a system that benefits both staff and the setting.
➤ Reveal the first sheet of paper on the flipchart and spend approximately ten minutes reading through the points together. Ask the staff to say what they think the positive impact of each point should be.

Preparation
➤ It would be useful to have undertaken the activities 'Appraisal and review' on page 108 and 'Using staff skills fully' on page 112 before carrying out this unit.
➤ Ask the staff to bring their completed confidential photocopiable sheets on page 156 or use your collated sections 4 and 5 from these sheets. Also, if possible, have copies of the completed photocopiable sheets on page 158.
➤ Ask the staff to bring their diaries and have your records of any past training or visits available.
➤ Prepare the flipchart as follows.
Sheet 1
The importance of staff professional development
Successful settings:
♦ recognise that continuous professional development is essential to keep them at the forefront of good practice
♦ ensure that they support their staff's professional development, matching both the setting's needs and those of the individual member of staff
♦ enable the staff to keep their practice fresh and to try new approaches

♦ plan and budget for a programme of staff development for all staff
♦ ensure that the staff disseminate ideas from their own training and visits to their colleagues
♦ give the staff opportunities to take a lead in projects and developments in the setting.
Sheet 2 (leave a space between headings)
Staff professional development:
♦ should be referred to in brochures, showing parents how your setting is forward thinking, with well-qualified staff
♦ should be recorded and shared with OFSTED inspectors, showing that professional development is planned for as part of your normal work
♦ should be formally recorded and shared with managers and governors, showing your setting's commitment to continuous improvement
♦ should be recorded in individual staff profiles, showing a record of personal professional development to support appraisal/Performance management and career advancement.
Sheet 3
A list of your current OFSTED key issues for development or identified priorities.

Sheet 4 (leave spaces between the questions)
A policy for disseminating external good practice
♦ What kinds of external good practice need sharing?
♦ How should we do this?
♦ Does it always need to be shared face to face?
♦ When should we do this?

➤ Stress that there are two layers of valuable professional development. Firstly, that individual members of staff can enjoy their own professional development through suitable training and opportunities, in order to reflect on their own and others' work. Secondly, and importantly, to ensure the steady overall improvement within your setting towards areas that have been identified for specific development.
➤ Now turn to the second sheet of paper on the flipchart. Explain that staff professional development, as a sign of a thriving and productive setting, should be communicated to a wide audience that need to be informed of your commitment to your staff and to sustaining and raising standards.
➤ Read through the headings together for approximately ten minutes. For each one, ask the staff how this might be carried out and add suggestions to the flipchart in a different coloured felt-tipped pen.
➤ Display the third sheet of paper on the flipchart and remind the staff of your setting's developmental areas. Now distribute a copy of the photocopiable sheet to each member of staff. Also give out your retained and completed photocopiable sheet on page 158.
➤ Explain that each member of staff should complete the new sheet

individually and that it will be included in a bank of staff development profiles. Agree the period to be covered and enter this.
➤ Now let the staff use the completed photocopiable sheet on page 158 plus their personal requests (from sections 4 and 5 of their 'Appraisal and review' sheet on page 156 to help them complete the top half of the page. Allow. approximately ten minutes for this.
➤ Then read through the columns and discuss the types of activity that should be included – external courses, visits to other settings, whole-setting training sessions, visiting speakers, discussions with teacher-mentors and/or other advisers and so on. Ask the staff to complete the photocopiable sheet within ten minutes, giving approximate dates if necessary, and collect these in.
➤ Focus on the 'Outcomes shared with colleagues' and make the point that, to be of the greatest value, ways should be found to report back to all the staff.
➤ For the remaining time, turn to the fourth sheet of paper on the flipchart. Read through the headings and discuss ideas. Write in agreed ways forward. Explain that this will form an important part of your staff development policy.

Further action
➤ Give each member of staff a copy of the completed sheets for their own record. Start a 'Staff development file' and include a set of sheets. Draw up a setting aggregated sheet showing main priorities with a list of staff training and development under each one. Put any extras under 'Other areas'. Write the dissemination policy and add this to the file. Share this aggregated sheet and policy with governors, managers and inspectors. Repeat the process annually.

Effective delegation

Focus on positive and productive procedures for delegating tasks

✿ Number of staff
All.

⏱ Timing
45 minutes.

What you need
A copy of the photocopiable sheet on page 160 for each member of staff; pens; enlarged copy of the photocopiable sheet; flipchart; felt-tipped pens; slips of paper; a list of any tasks to be delegated, possibly from other training units in this book.

What you do
➤ Explain that the aim of this session is to agree procedures for delegating important developments effectively so that results are positive and productive.
➤ Make a strong statement that all good teams, especially small ones, need to delegate tasks to team members in order to share out the workload and capitalise on strengths. Give examples of where this has gone well in your setting in the past.
➤ Look at the first sheet on paper on the flipchart. Read through the

Preparation
➤ It would be useful to have undertaken the activity 'Using staff skills fully' on page 112 before carrying out this unit as this should result in key tasks being identified for all the staff.
➤ Write the members of staff's names on to the slips of paper and add any task that is to be delegated.
➤ Prepare the flipchart as follows.

Sheet 1
A cautionary tale
At the Sunshine nursery school the manager has decided to develop parental involvement in the setting. Mary Jane, an enthusiastic and energetic member of staff, has been asked by her manager to explore ways of increasing the numbers of active parents in school.

She has a lot of ideas and sends out a letter to all parents asking them to attend a meeting. Many parents attend and Mary Jane 'signs them up' to come into school to help. Several arrive unexpectedly the very next day but staff are unprepared and rather fraught.

Parents do not feel welcomed or useful and indicate they will not come again. Staff feel upset by the unplanned influx of parents and their response.

Other parents have written to complain to the manager that they can't help in school as they need to work and say that they were made to feel awkward by Mary Jane's letter. The manager is angry as she knew nothing about the letter or meeting. She remonstrates Mary Jane about her handling of the situation. Whoops!
What has gone wrong and how could it have been avoided? How could it be put right?

Sheet 2
What makes for effective delegation?
When we are asked to lead a new development, or carry out a task, what do we need to know?

Sheet 3
What makes for effective delegation?
When we ask someone to lead a new development, or carry out a task, what do we need to clarify with them?

case study together and then ask the staff to work in pairs or small groups and spend ten minutes making a list of what went wrong and why this was. Also ask how the problems could have been avoided and how things might be put right.

➤ Invite everyone to feedback their ideas and spend approximately ten minutes discussing their responses.

➤ Present the second sheet of paper on the flipchart. Ask the staff to suggest the key features of delegation for a person who is asked to carry out, or lead a particular project. Spend approximately five minutes in discussion and ask a member of staff to write the staff's ideas on the sheet.

➤ Turn to the third sheet of paper on the flipchart and repeat the activity, this time looking at the key features for the person who is doing the delegating. Take a further five minutes for discussion and invite a scribe to add the staff's suggestions to the sheet.

➤ Now reveal the enlarged copy of the photocopiable sheet. Read through the headings and stress how important it is in the delegation process for all parties to be clear about what has to be done – when and how people will be informed and how progress will be reported.

➤ As a group, using the ideas on the last two sheets, fill in as much of the delegation sheet as you can. You can make up dates and names to help! Take ten minutes for this task.

➤ Now give a copy of the photocopiable sheet to each member of staff and, if possible, a slip with an area they have agreed to take responsibility for. (If this is not possible, let the staff work in groups to help someone who has been delegated a task, or make up some imaginary projects.) Allow at least

ten minutes for this activity.

➤ Invite the staff to feed back on their delegation sheets.

➤ Finally, stress that with real projects, the manager would need to arrange a brief meeting for discussing and clarifying an individual's ideas, needs and dates. Both members of staff would then sign the final agreed form and each have a copy for their reference.

Further action

➤ Arrange a programme of short interviews with all the staff with delegated responsibilities and ask them to present their completed sheets. Agree the details and countersign them, putting key dates and times in diaries and making any arrangements to inform anyone affected by the project. Ensure that all agreed resources, including staff time, are planned for appropriately.

➤ Add a copy of the agreed delegation sheet to the 'Staff development file' (see the activity 'Developing staff profiles' on page 116) as leadership of projects can constitute valuable professional development.

➤ Make a composite list for the staffroom noticeboard of all delegated projects including lead and support staff, time-scales and implications for other staff.

A check-list for your setting concerning the issues raised in **Chapter 8** Staff development

➤ Do we have a staff development policy for our setting?

➤ Have we got a system that enables everyone to review their personal work on a regular basis?

➤ How do we ensure that all the staff, irrespective of their roles, have opportunities to discuss their work privately on an individual basis?

➤ Do we build in time for all the staff to reflect on what they do well or need to develop more?

➤ How do we enable the staff to identify what further training they might need?

➤ Have we set up a staff training budget?

➤ Who decides who can access training?

➤ How do we know if it is value for money?

➤ What positive difference has staff development made to our work?

➤ Is everyone guaranteed some form of staff development?

➤ How does this work in practice?

➤ Do we look at different ways of tackling staff development (such as visits, visiting colleagues, whole staff 'in-house' training, teacher-mentor sessions, courses and conferences)?

➤ How many of these approaches do we use?

➤ How do we get feedback from the staff who have been on external training?

➤ Would an appraisal and review system be valuable in our setting?

➤ What are the benefits of a Performance management system for our setting?

➤ How might we design a personalised and workable programme for our setting?

➤ Who would act as team leaders?

➤ What other training might we need before embarking on this?

➤ Do we know what special skills, interests and experience all the staff have?

➤ Do we review this regularly enough?

➤ How do we capitalise on staff skills and interests?

➤ How do we help the staff to widen their experience and try new things?

➤ How can we work more effectively as a team?

➤ In which areas do we work well as a team?

➤ What gets in the way of us working really well as a team?

➤ How can we minimise any problems?

➤ Do we have staff profiles?

➤ How do these function?

➤ How frequently are these used and updated?

➤ How might we inform parents about our commitment to staff development?

➤ How do we show OFSTED inspectors that we take staff development seriously?

➤ Do we have a balance of personal professional development and whole-staff development to address our setting's aims for improvement?

➤ Do all the staff have a chance to take responsibility for aspects of work or specific projects?

➤ How good are our delegation procedures?

➤ Is everyone clear what they have to do and to whom they report and when?

Staff training activities

early years
*training &
management*

Auditing your coverage of the six Areas of Learning

Area of Learning

Early Learning Goal

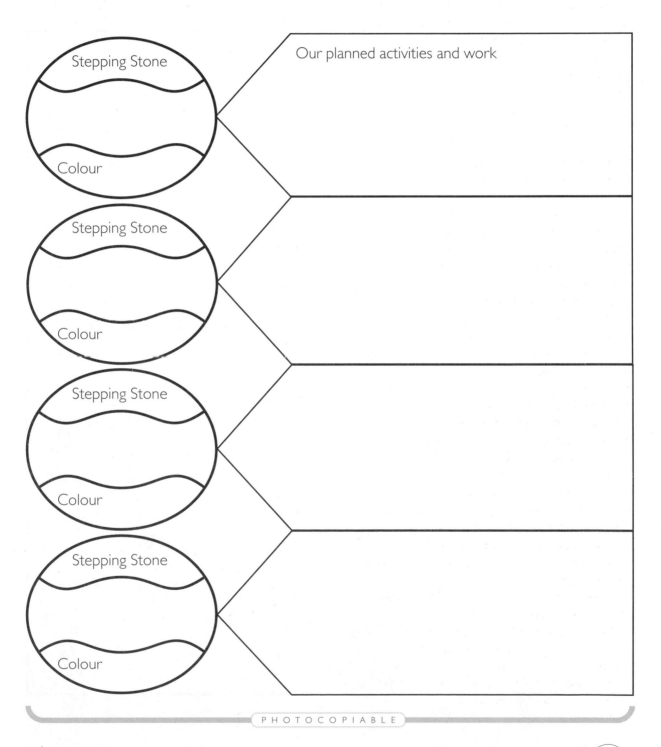

Stepping Stone

Colour

Stepping Stone

Colour

Stepping Stone

Colour

Stepping Stone

Colour

Our planned activities and work

Introducing new ideas successfully

YES! This idea will succeed because…	**MAYBE NOT!** This idea may not suceed because…
The benefits will be…	The problems will be…
The Enthusiast	The Worrier
To make it succeed we'll need these Resources…	**To make it suceed we'll need to. . .**
Because…	Because…
The Resource Manager	The Organiser

Involving the team fully

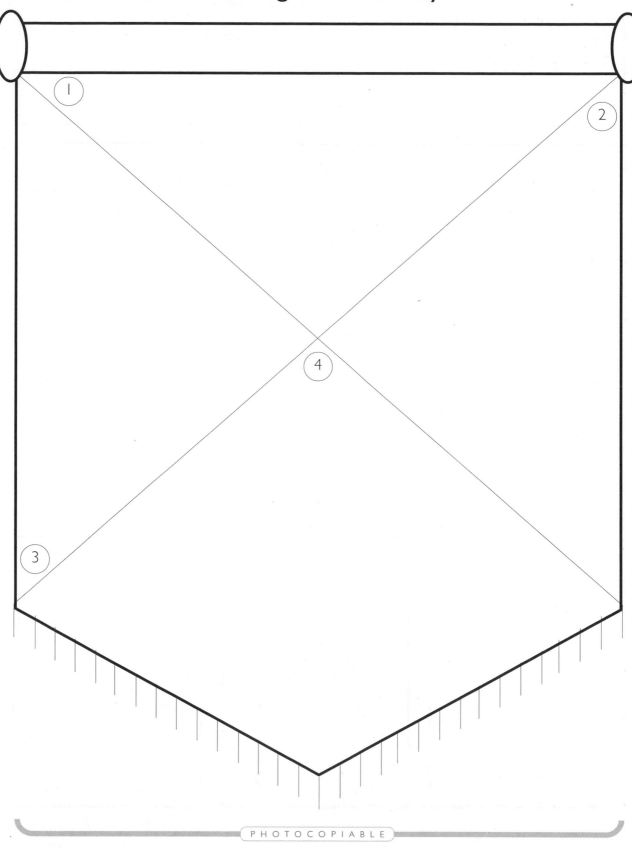

early years
**training &
management** Staff training activities

📖 SCHOLASTIC 123

Developing our provision for play

Play activity _____ Date _____

Linked with _____ Topic/theme _____

Areas of Learning addressed _____

Personal, social and emotional development	Communication, language and literacy	Mathematical development
How? Intervention? Resources?	How? Intervention? Resources?	How? Intervention? Resources?
Knowledge and understanding of the world	**Physical development**	**Creative development**
How? Intervention? Resources?	How? Intervention? Resources?	How? Intervention? Resources?

PHOTOCOPIABLE

Staff training activities *early years* **training & management**

Planning for the future

Plan the Areas of Learning that will be covered and how this will be done.

What needs to be done?	Who will do it? (Lead/Support)	How will we do it?	When? (Start/Finish)	What resources will we need?	How will we know it's been successful?

Observation techniques

Key questions _____ Date _____

Who was observed?

Which activity was observed?

Was the observation planned or incidental?

What was observed? Who was involved?

Which Areas of Learning were involved?

What learning took place?

To extend learning further, we shall need to…

PHOTOCOPIABLE

**SCHOLASTIC

Staff training activities

early years
*training &
management*

Staff involvement

Complete the jigsaw pieces with titles for your setting, then fill in the details.

The teacher's role in assessment should be…

_____'s role in assessment should be…

_____'s role in assessment should be…

_____'s role in assessment should be…

_____'s role in assessment should be…

The headteacher's/ manager's role in assessment should be…

The parents' role in assessment could be…

_____'s role in assessment should be…

The helpers' role in assessment could be…

Recording initial profiling

Complete the balloons with your observations and sources of evidence.

Communication, language and literacy

Mathematical development

Knowledge and understanding of the world

Creative development

Physical development

Personal, social and emotional development

Other useful information required

Staff training activities

early years
training & management

Sharing with parents

Interview a colleague in role as a new parent and complete the form.

Child's name _____ Date of birth _____

Position in family _____

Name of parent or guardian _____

Any access arrangements _____

Special medical conditions (asthma, eczema, allergies and so on) _____

Any physical conditions/considerations (glasses, hearing and so on) _____

Special interests, likes and skills _____

Dislikes _____

Special friends _____

Favourite toys _____

Pets _____

Any other issues _____

PHOTOCOPIABLE

early years training & management Staff training activities

Using assessment information to promote learning

Child's name _____ · Date _____

Further support needed to help him/her _____

Complete the planning wall with your intentions. Complete the 'Outcome' after the activity.

How this could be done

Area of Learning	Early Learning Goal/Stepping Stone

How long?	Planned activity	When?

Who will be involved?	Resources	Outcome

Staff training activities *early years* **training & management**

Auditing our resources and learning environment

Consider the quality of your resources and surrounding learning area and complete the boxes.

Sand and water play	Small-world play	Technology and construction equipment
✔ (good) ✘ (poor) Needs	✔ ✘ Needs	✔ ✘ Needs
Table-top games/kits	Outdoor-play equipment	Home and role-play resources
✔ ✘ Needs	✔ ✘ Needs	✔ ✘ Needs
Creative development resources	Physical development resources	Other areas
✔ ✘ Needs	✔ ✘ Needs	✔ ✘ Needs

PHOTOCOPIABLE

Extending learning through quality play

Play area _____

Current use _____

Future use _____

Related topic/theme _____

Add your ideas for a focus, resources to stimulate learning, and ways to develop play aspects related to your theme.

Staff training activities   early years
training &
management

The balance of directed and independent work

Directed activity

Activity _____

What I want children to learn (skills, knowledge, understanding)

_____

Resources _____

Intervention ideas (questions, vocabulary, extension, challenge)

Activity _____

Stimulus _____

Choices (range, free, limitations) _____

Resources (space, time, equipment) _____

Opportunities for children's choice and initiative

Displays with impact

Review the displays in your setting and complete the sheet.

Do displays extend learning enough?

Strengths:
Weaknesses:

Can we see work from children of different abilities?

More able?   Less able?
Average?   SEN?

How much work is from children? From adults?

What is the balance overall?

Which Areas of Learning are featured?

Do we have enough titles? Headings? Questions?

Strengths
Weaknesses

Is literacy prominent enough? Numeracy?

Strengths
Weaknesses

Where are our multicultural dimensions?

◗ SCHOLASTIC

Staff training activities   early years training & management

Maximising the quality of outdoor learning

fixed apparatus — tents — roadways — tree hides — mazes

wildlife areas — parking bays — fixed black and white boards — playground markings — logs and tables

art installations — musical instruments — outdoor classroom — role-play — houses and shops

Write outdoor play suggestions on the petals, cut out and display.

gardening — climbing — minibeast hunts — observing

early years training & management   Staff training activities

📖 SCHOLASTIC

Developing parental partnerships

Good ideas bank

Develop a home links pack for new parents – consult 'older' parents for ideas.

Arrange parent and child taster visits – sharing sessions.

Involve parents in compiling children's personal files, home information.

Extend home visits and/or pre-induction sessions.

Develop home learning packs and ideas (books, toys, games, tasks).

Start/develop parents' newsletters and year books.

Start our curriculum information move
– posters
– booklets
– topics

Have a parents' tea and information party – seek parents' views more.

Link with training for adults, providers and offer courses.

Have a drive to recruit more parent helpers – it's cool to contribute!

In our setting we could…

BANK OF GOOD IDEAS

BANK OF GOOD IDEAS

BANK OF GOOD IDEAS

SCHOLASTIC

Staff training activities · early years *training & management*

Good communications

Type of communication	Yes	Requires development	No	Comments
We send out regular **newsletters.**				
They include children's work				
They include photographs.				
They are bright and attractive.				
They are personalised to our setting.				
We have good **induction information**.				
Our brochure is attractive and informative.				
Our brochure is personalised well.				
We build in individual discussions with parents.				
We have productive home visits.				
We have productive pre-entry visits to our setting.				
We **inform parents about our curriculum**.				
The noticeboard gives useful curriculum information.				
Parents know how to help their children with their learning.				
We invite **parents' comments.**				
We use videos, displays and so on.				
We consult/use mother tongue on information.				

Working with parents in the setting

Parent helper card

Date _____

Please help with the _____ activity

Your group will be

What they need to do

What they should learn

Please stress this vocabulary

Community links

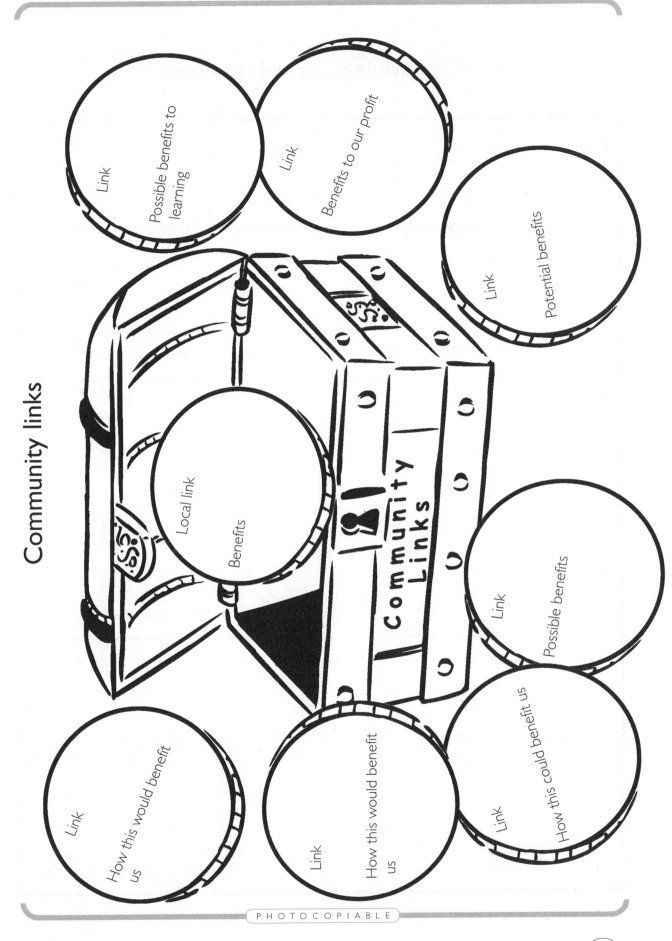

Link
Possible benefits to learning

Link
Benefits to our profit

Link
Potential benefits

Local link
Benefits

Community Links

Link
Possible benefits

Link
How this would benefit us

Link
How this would benefit us

Link
How this could benefit us

Developing our self-review

Complete the triangles for each Area of Learning.

+ What we do *really* well

+ What we do *really* well

Personal, social and emotional development

Communication, language and literacy

– What needs development

– What needs development

+ What we do *really* well

+ What we do *really* well

Mathematical development

Knowledge and understanding of the world

– What needs development

– What needs development

+ What we do *really* well

+ What we do *really* well

Creative development

Physical development

– What needs development

– What needs development

  SCHOLASTIC

Staff training activities

early years
*training &
management*

Identifying and sharing best practice

Review area _____

Discuss best practice and complete the sheet (in groups).

How well do we do it? Examples of our best practice	The impact on children's learning?
How well do others do it? Good practice examples	Likely impact on children's learning?
We would like to find out more about	Make visits to

Identifying areas for development

Review the work sample and complete the sheet.

Average (A)	Below average (BA)	Above average (AA)
Overall progress	Overall progress	Overall progress
More attention needed to	More attention needed to	More attention needed to
Average (A)	Below average (BA)	Above average (AA)
Overall progress	Overall progress	Overall progress
More attention needed to	More attention needed to	More attention needed to
Average (A)	Below average (BA)	Above average (AA)
Overall progress	Overall progress	Overall progress
More attention needed to	More attention needed to	More attention needed to

Age group

Age group

Age group

Further evidence we need

SCHOLASTIC

Staff training activities

early years
*training &
management*

Reviewing our teaching and learning

Proposed teaching activity

What do I want the children
- To learn?
- To experience?
- To improve?

- To understand?
- To be able to do?
- To know?

How will I organise the session?

How long will it take?

Resources I will need

How will I know they have made progress?

Key vocabulary to share

Evaluation and review

How did it go?

What I need to do next

early years
training & management

Staff training activities

■ SCHOLASTIC

Sharing best practice together

Prepare for your presentation on an aspect of your best practice by completing the 'script'.

BEST PRACTICE

Working with (children)

Activity

What I wanted them to learn

What I did

Outcomes to learning

What was really successful and why

Problems I encountered

How I solved them

What I might do differently next time

  SCHOLASTIC

Staff training activities — early years **training & management**

Visit preparation

Area of focus _____ What I want to find out What I will look for on my visit Other information I will need How can I find this out?	**Pre-visit preparation**
What I saw on my visit Ideas to discuss and develop in our setting	**Post-visit report**

PHOTOCOPIABLE

Preparing for re-inspection
(Primary and nursery schools)

Previous inspection (date)

What needed attention

What we are doing about it

Whole school issues

What we've done about it

What still needs to be done

SCHOLASTIC

Staff training activities

early years
*training &
management*

Preparing for re-inspection
(Private, voluntary and independent settings)

Characteristics of our setting	Changes
Previous inspection (date)	How good is our provision now?
How good was our provision?	
Personal, social and emotional development	
Communication, language and literacy	How good is our parental partnership now?
Mathematical development	
Knowledge and understanding of the world	What have we done about it?
Creative development	
Physical development	What are we doing about it now?
How good was our parental partnership?	
What did we need to do next?	What do we still need to do?

Positive approaches to weaknesses

Areas that need attention

1 _____   3 _____

2 _____   4 _____

Cut out the flags, add suggestions and arrange them in order of action.

Steps forward	Steps forward
Area_____	Area_____
Area	Area
Steps forward	Steps forward
Steps forward	Steps forward
Area_____	Area_____
Area	Area
Steps forward	Steps forward

◖ SCHOLASTIC

Staff training activities

early years
*training &
management*

Dealing with the inspection visit

Ready for Inspection health check-list	Yes	Partly	No
1 Have I planned all the activities taking place during the inspection?			
2 Do all the activities have clear learning objectives?			
3 Are all the support staff and helpers informed and ready?			
4 Have I checked and organised all the resources?			
5 Is my planning ready for scrutiny?			
6 Are my records up to date and in good order?			
7 Have I got a clear idea of how I shall organise groups?			
8 Have I planned who will work with specific children and when?			
9 Is my area neatly organised, with the resources to hand? Have I cleared away any clutter?			
10 Are the displays varied, stimulating and likely to extend learning?			
11 Is the area likely to support literacy and numeracy?			
12 Have I got evidence for the inspectors of a broad range of work, including Areas of Learning not obvious during the inspection?			
13 Are the home/role-play areas clean, well labelled and exciting?			
14 Is outdoor play fully exploited during the inspection?			
15 Do I know how I shall support children with SEN and EAL?			
16 Have I shared all my intentions with my colleagues?			

PHOTOCOPIABLE

early years
training & management   Staff training activities

◖SCHOLASTIC

Action plans

Post-inspection action plan

Setting _____

People involved in
creating this plan _____

Date _____

Review date _____

Issue to be addressed (key issues from the report)	Strategies (how it will be done)	Personnel (who will do it)	Time-scale (when it will be done)	Resources/costs/ equipment	Monitored by (who will check it happens)	Success criteria (we will be successful when…)

◖SCHOLASTIC

Staff training activities   early years *training & management*

Equal opportunities audit

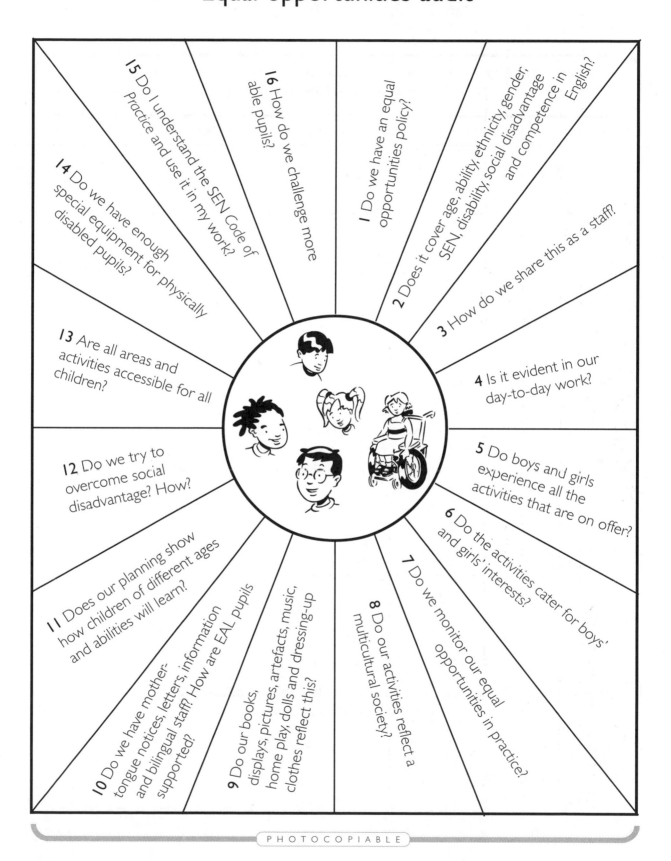

15 Do I understand the SEN Code of practice and use it in my work?

16 How do we challenge more able pupils?

1 Do we have an equal opportunities policy?

2 Does it cover age, ability, ethnicity, gender, SEN, disability, social disadvantage and competence in English?

14 Do we have enough special equipment for physically disabled pupils?

3 How do we share this as a staff?

13 Are all areas and activities accessible for all children?

4 Is it evident in our day-to-day work?

12 Do we try to overcome social disadvantage? How?

5 Do boys and girls experience all the activities that are on offer?

11 Does our planning show how children of different ages and abilities will learn?

6 Do the activities cater for boys' and girls' interests?

10 Do we have mother-tongue notices, letters, information and bilingual staff? How are EAL pupils supported?

9 Do our books, displays, pictures, artefacts, music, home play, dolls and dressing-up clothes reflect this?

8 Do our activities reflect a multicultural society?

7 Do we monitor our equal opportunities in practice?

Developing inclusion in the curriculum

Activities – role-play – books – stories – resources – displays – circle time – costumes – behaviour codes – targeted learning

Look at your next week's planning and note how you will support specific issues in your work.

Gender issues — how will we support boys and girls specifically?

Physical disability issues — how will children be helped to access all activities?

Ethnic group issues — how will we support these groups?
— how will we promote racial harmony?
— how will we prepare children for living in a culturally diverse society?

Ability issues — how will we support children of different abilities and ages?

Behaviour issues — how will we manage undesirable behaviour?
— how will we promote good behaviour?

Staff training activities   *early years* **training & management**

Implementing the SEN *Code of Practice*

Complete the grids.

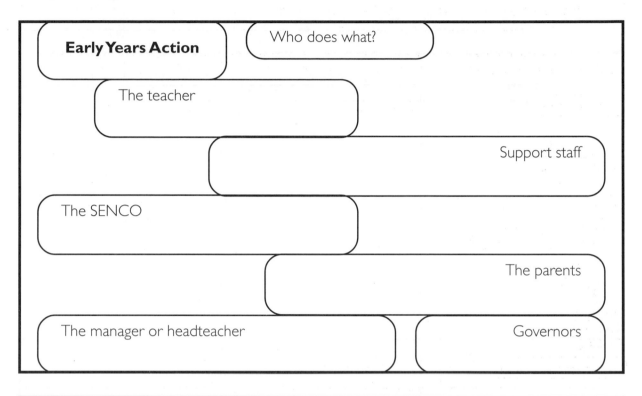

Early Years Action   Who does what?

The teacher

Support staff

The SENCO

The parents

The manager or headteacher   Governors

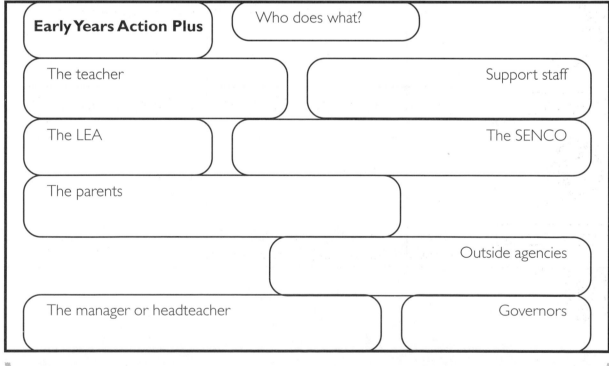

Early Years Action Plus   Who does what?

The teacher   Support staff

The LEA   The SENCO

The parents

Outside agencies

The manager or headteacher   Governors

Working with parents and other agencies

Prepare for a review meeting by completing the sheet.

Child's name _____ Date of birth _____

Date of review _____

Assessment, planning and review	Outcomes/evidence	Further action
Grouping for teaching purposes	Outcomes/evidence	Further action
Additional human resources	Outcomes/evidence	Further action
Curriculum and teaching methods	Outcomes/evidence	Further action
Parents' views		

Staff training activities early years *training & management*

Supporting children with SEN

Complete the planning sheet for individual pupils.

Child's name _____ Age _____ Class _____

Nature of SEN

Early Years Action   What does the IEP say?

Targets?

Teaching strategies?

Provision?

Review date?

Outcome of previous reviews?

How could I plan to meet learning needs?

What specific observations/records do I need?

What are the parents' and child's views?

Appraisal and review

CONFIDENTIAL

Name _____ Position _____ Date _____

Specific roles and responsibilities

I _____

These areas of my work have been successful this year…

Because…

I am especially proud of…

Because…

2 _____

What wasn't so successful…

Because…

3 _____

Next year I really would like to…

4 _____

How my manager could help me develop…

5 _____

Performance management

Reflect on these elements of Performance management and decide how these might benefit your setting.

Elements and reflections	PRO and why	CON and why
A Performance management system would benefit our setting		
It should apply to all staff		
It should apply only to specific staff		
A children's progress target would be useful for all staff		
A children's progress target would be useful for staff		
Personal responsibility targets would be useful for all staff		
Individual professional development targets would give everyone a chance to follow follow personal needs.		
Observations and feedback of our work with children will be useful to us.		
Team leaders would work well here		
The manager should do all Performance management elements		
We need more Performance management training together managementtraining together.		
Performance management must be confidential		
Other comments		

PHOTOCOPIABLE

Using staff skills fully

Complete the sections to give your skills/interests profile.

I think I am really good at…

I really enjoy…

Interests, hobbies, sports, talents OUTSIDE work…

In our setting, I should like to…

I am interested in finding out more about/visiting…

◆SCHOLASTIC

Staff training activities · early years **training & management**

Staff development profile

Name _____ Position _____

Period _____ To _____

The school/setting training/development areas

1 _____

2 _____

3 _____

4 _____

5 _____

Personal training/development areas

1 _____

2 _____

3 _____

Date	Course/training followed	Visits/research	Outcomes shared with colleagues

Staff training activities

SCHOLASTIC 159

Effective delegation

Complete the details then check it with your manager.

(What I am going to do)

(How will it be done)

Start	Review progress with manager	Completed

(When it will be done)

Resources	Help from	To inform	Time

(The successful outcome will be . . .)

Discussed and agreed on _____ (date)

Signed (Staff) _____

(Manager) _____

Comments